THE RICK & BUBBA CODE

By

Rick Burgess
and
Bill "Bubba" Bussey

with Martha Bolton

THOMAS NELSON
Since 1798

NASHVILLE   DALLAS   MEXICO CITY   RIO DE JANEIRO   BEIJING

Published in Nashville, TN, by Thomas Nelson. Thomas Nelson is a trademark of Thomas Nelson, Inc.

Thomas Nelson, Inc., titles may be purchased in bulk for educational, business, fundraising, or sales promotional use. For information, please e-mail SpecialMarkets@ThomasNelson.com.

All scripture quotations, unless otherwise indicated, are taken from The Holy Bible, New International Version. Copyright © 1973, 1978, 1984. International Bible Society. Used by permission of Zondervan Bible Publishers.

Library of Congress Cataloging-in-Publication Data

ISBN-10 0-8499-1877-4
ISBN-13 978-0-8499-1877-3

Printed in the United States of America

07 08 09 10 11 12 RRD 5 4 3 2 1

This book is dedicated to our number one earthly priorities—
our wives, Sherri and Betty, along with our children who
make each day an adventure worth living.

CONTENTS

CONTENTS

CONTENTS

ACKNOWLEDGMENTS

We would like to thank, first and foremost, the one and only living GOD who loved us so much that he sent his only son JESUS CHRIST to die in our place; through his grace we are forgiven. Thank you God for sending the world's greatest hero, our Savior Jesus Christ.

We would also like to thank:
 Our wives, Sherri and Betty, for their love and support

Our children:
 Rick: Brandi, Blake, Brooks, Brody, and Bronner
 Bubba: Hunter and Katelyn

Our staff:
 Calvin "Speedy" Wilburn
 Don Juan Demarco Williams
 Ryan Greenwood
 The Interns: Past, Present and Future
 Jim Dunaway
 Ken "Bones" Hearns

All of our friends who support us and hold us accountable:
 Martha Bolton, the staff at Thomas Nelson, and David Sanford
 The entire Rick and Bubba Radio Family

The greatest, most influential, best-looking listening audience in the world! Wow, you are a blessing and you make getting up early worth it!

FACTS

▸ Rick and Bubba's first book, *Rick and Bubba's Expert Guide to God, Country, Family and Anything Else We Can Think Of* debuted in the number one spot on Amazon and booksamillion.com, and hit #7 on the *New York Times* bestseller list.

▸ Rick and Bubba have spent all of the money from that book.

▸ Rick and Bubba would love for this book to sell just as well as their first one.

▸ Rick and Bubba are not above begging friends, family, and fans to buy this book. (After all, it worked last time. It's not easy to claim that number one spot on Amazon. And they did it . . . right behind a toaster oven.)

▸ Rick and Bubba will accept food (preferably fried) in exchange for an autographed copy of this book.

▸ Rick and Bubba belong to a secret society known as Early Bird Diners.

▸ Rick and Bubba once saw the *Mona Lisa*. Not the real one. A cartoon where animators made the lips move.

▸ Rick and Bubba are about to divulge all the mysteries of life that have, until now, been safely locked away in their minds (and on a soiled Chick-Fil-A napkin carbon dated 1987).

▸ Rick and Bubba continue to reign unchallenged as the "Two Sexiest Fat Men Alive."

PROLOGUE

Undisclosed Radio Station, Birmingham, Alabama
6:30 a.m.

A *while back . . .*

Renowned radio archivist Calvin "Speedy" Wilburn staggers by the Big Boy statue in the parking lot of The Rick and Bubba Show *in Birmingham, Alabama. He enters the building, reaching for the nearest photo he can see. It's radio personalities Rick and Bubba at a local fish fry—a Kodak shot. Grabbing the frame, Speedy pulls the photo toward him until it rips off the wall (Velcro always releases with the right amount of pressure). The weight of the frame knocks him to the ground.*

Writhing in pain, Speedy gathers up all his courage and stamina. The job before him: to unveil the secrets of The Rick and Bubba Code *to the world, secrets that have been hidden for thousands of years—or at least a couple of weeks—is daunting. The gravity of the situation weighs as heavy in his stomach as a double cheeseburger with onions. And chili fries. In other words, Rick and Bubba's usual breakfast. This mission will surely take every one of the last remaining moments of his life.*

Or not.

Maybe he can just get Rick and Bubba to put it all down in another bestselling book and go on with his life. Maybe, just maybe, there is still hope. . . .

Wherever You Happen to Be.
Present Time.
Present Day.

This volume of secrets you hold in your hand could not be unveiled before today. Why, you ask? These secrets hold power that potentially can alter the course of history. Or at the very least, can alter Rick and Bubba's bank account balance to the plus column. Yes, society has long believed certain truths to be rock solid, but *The Rick and Bubba Code* is about to expose the conspiracy that has kept the real truth hidden for so long.

Now, the entire world may know exactly what has been discovered in the long hidden Rick and Bubba Code. Some of these closely guarded secrets are too mysterious for even Rick and Bubba to understand.

But that hasn't stopped this heroic duo from telling them.

THE
RICK &
BUBBA
CODE

PART I

DECODING MEN AND WOMEN

For any of you who may not have noticed it yet, there are a few differences between men and women. Major differences. We're equal, of course, but we're different. We also happen to believe that women have the edge. Not a lot, but in our relatively short duration here on earth, we have learned first-hand that there are certain disadvantages to being a man.

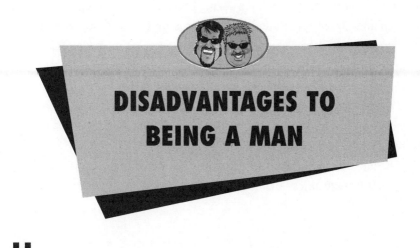

DISADVANTAGES TO BEING A MAN

Here's just a portion of the ever-accumulating list.

1. In an emergency, it's "Women and children first."

Who made up this rule? Obviously a woman. Or a child. It certainly couldn't have been a man. After all, man was created to survive. It's the "survival of the fittest," not the "demise of the most polite." We suspect some woman probably made up this rule during some long-ago emergency, and the men standing around at the time were too weak to object.

We are not weak men. In fact, whenever I (Rick) am on an airplane, I always look around and make sure I'm in a position where I can take anybody that's between me and one of the exit doors. I realize this sounds a bit self-centered, but it's simply survival instincts. It's also for the greater good of the others on the plane. I know if I can get out of that airplane first, then I'll be in a position to run to a nearby farmhouse, have a soda, and then call 911. (In an emergency situation I have been known to drink an entire can of soda in five seconds flat.) The rescue team would be on its way for the others in no time at all.

Another reason why I should be the first one off the plane is because when the elderly lady sitting in the emergency row next to me starts shoving the passengers out the door and down that big yellow slide, there needs to be someone at the bottom who is strong enough to catch them. I couldn't let women and children just tumble down an emergency chute with no one down there to catch them. That's not the kind of stock I'm made of. I would stand there dutifully waiting for that first big guy to come sliding down and then assign him the job while I looked for my luggage.

It would work the same if I were on a cruise ship. If I have to knock a few others out of the way so I can get into the lifeboat first in order to help those behind me, well, then so be it.

Never let it be said that Rick Burgess wasn't willing to put his safety first for the ultimate safety of the masses.

2. Men have to take out the garbage.

Again, who decided that this would be the man's job? The bottom of the bag can rip open just as easily for us as it can for our wives. We're not even the ones filling the bags either. Our trash rarely makes it into the trash containers in the first place. Should the pain of all those missed "baskets" be compounded with having to haul the trash bags out to the curb, too?

Like other men, taking out the garbage is my (Bubba) job. And like other men, I didn't even get a vote. Every Monday morning it is incumbent upon me to see that the garbage cans make it to the street. According to the Betty Bussey Family Proclamation, I handle everything outside the house; she handles everything inside the house. But the garbage cans, which are technically both inside and outside the house, have been declared my responsibility. There's no bucking it: It's written in ink, with calligraphy.

For years I operated under the mistaken assumption that writing a book and having a radio and television show was a big deal to my wife. I have since learned it is not. In fact, when our first book came out, Betty lovingly said, "That's wonderful, honey. But you're still rolling the trash can to the street!"

If this book sells a million copies, it will still be, "That's wonderful, honey. But you're still rolling the trash can to the street!"

If I win the Nobel Prize for literature, she will send a note up to me right in the middle of my acceptance speech, reminding me that my true calling involves cans filled with banana peels, Twinkie wrappers, and toilet paper rolls.

After all, Betty takes this job of mine seriously. It doesn't matter how successful I become in life. In the end, my total worth will be judged (as it is each week) by one standard alone: whether or not I have taken out the garbage.

3. There are no sofas in men's restrooms.

Okay, ladies, this one's a fairness issue. Each of us has accidentally walked into enough of your restrooms to know that we men are being shortchanged in the public restroom department. Your facilities are clean, some smell like flowers or sea breezes, and a good number of them have sofas. This is in addition to working toilets, filled soap and paper dispensers, faucets that you can turn on and off, and the occasional bottle of hand lotion.

Men don't get any of that. The attendant checklist on the wall of the average men's restroom has a last entry of June 12, 1998; the soap dispenser will be empty and crusted over; the faucet—if it's even running—will squirt water in six different directions; and you will never ever find anything that even resembles a sofa.

As for aromas, our status as Southern gentlemen keeps us from going into detail. Just know this: if you've ever wondered why men's restroom lines move a lot faster than women's, the answer is simple—a man can only hold his breath for so long.

4. Even if we fall from thirty-foot scaffolding, we are not supposed to cry.

I don't know who made up the rule about men not being allowed to cry, but again, not fair. The fairer Kleenex-toting sex has known for centuries that sometimes in life, you just have to cry. After all, you can't watch your team lose the Super Bowl by a field goal and not show some sort of emotion. And you should see us bawling every April 15th.

The fact of the matter is, we (Rick and Bubba) do cry. And we're man enough to admit it.

5. Unlike women, we can't flirt our way out of a traffic ticket.

A cop pulls a pretty girl over for running a stop sign. The girl smiles (or cries), bats her eyelashes a few times, and the cop might let her off with a warning. This same cop pulls a guy over for the exact same infraction . . . and it's life with no chance of parole.

6. We have to take orders from women.

All our lives it seems that we men have been taking orders from a woman. When we were young, we took them from our moms. When we grew up and got married, we started answering to our wives. Now for me (Bubba), it's my cute little seven-year-old daughter, Katelyn, who is starting to order me around. My goal in life is to someday be the one in charge before I die. . . . that is if it's okay with my mom, Betty, and Katelyn.

Note: We originally planned to have twenty items on this list, but we couldn't finish it. Bubba had to take out the trash, and Rick's wife said that six was plenty.

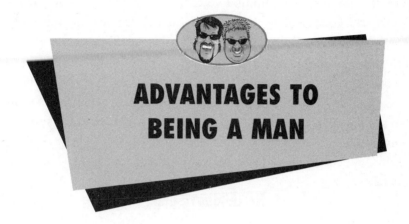

ADVANTAGES TO BEING A MAN

Don't get us wrong. There are some advantages to being men.

1. No one expects men to grow up.

No one looks twice at a man still playing with video games into his forties and fifties. In fact, the best thing that adulthood did to us was get us a job where we could buy our own big screen TVs to play our video games on. This is totally acceptable in society.

Not true for a woman. If a forty-five-year-old woman were to pull out her EZ Bake oven and start trying to cook a roast for dinner, we'd send her off for an evaluation. And some take-out food. We don't want to see our wives standing over a stove that's half her height, baking us a cake the size of a cookie. We want her using a real kitchen and making us a real dinner after our hard day of . . . watching football and playing video games.

2. You get to be the fun parent.

For many men, their duties in childrearing are lighter so there's more free time to play. Moms—not all mind you, but most—are better at teaching the lessons of good hygiene and manners and at keeping the kids somewhat presentable. A Dad's strengths lie in the tickling and wrestling department.

If our kids don't remember anything else, we want them to be able to say one day, "Dad played with me." We think every kid secretly hopes that he can say that about his or her father. That, and that he was the strongest and smartest man in the world.

3. No childbirth pain.

This is a great advantage to being a male. Our part in producing offspring is, well, a lot more fun than childbirth. We don't have to go through the pain of labor. We may be there in the room for the birthing process, but when it's all over, we just scoop up the baby and do the touchdown dance without breaking a sweat. Our poor wife, worn out from some twelve hours of hard labor, can barely lift her head, and we're sitting on the side of the bed complaining that the air conditioning's a little cool and could the nurse turn it down a notch or two.

Don't be misled, though. We men don't escape all pain during childbirth. Our cheek muscles get pretty sore from helping with all that Lamaze breathing, as well as from our wives pinching our faces as they turn it from the TV back toward them and say, "Quit watching that game and pay attention!"

4. Style is not as important.

We men can wear khaki shorts and a jersey every day of our lives and we're happy. Or our favorite pair of sweats. Or even a shirt from the sixties. We have learned to be content in "whatsoever state we're in." We don't need a bunch of pairs of shoes either. I (Rick) have just three pairs of shoes: tennis shoes, beach sandals, and Sunday shoes. No matter what Paris Hilton thinks or how often she shops, three pairs of shoes are all any of us really need.

5. We can open jars, in most cases, without bringing in the dynamite.

Emphasis on "in most cases." We're not sure what they're sealing pickle jars with these days, but NASA ought to be looking into it for their spaceships.

6. Men don't have unrealistic expectations of themselves.

Unlike girls and their Barbies, guys have never taken the Ken doll seriously. Guys don't grow up thinking that's what we have to look like to be successful in life. No grown man is walking around saying, "If I could just be more like Ken." When's the last time you saw Ken designer clothes for men in a department store? As far as we know, no one is marketing Ken Dream Garages or Ken Corvettes to us men. No man is in therapy today because of what living up to the Ken image did to him in his childhood. Nor is he starving himself because he doesn't have the same chiseled chest or waistline as the Ken doll. We just don't get caught up in trying to meet an impossible standard. Barbie's pretty, but it's an unattainable goal, ladies. Do you have any idea how many Hershey bars you'd have to pass up to have a two-inch waistline?

7. Our last name doesn't change when we marry.

This can be a huge advantage, especially for bachelors who own monogrammed towels that still have some threads left in them.

8. Overweight, average-looking men can marry stunningly beautiful women.

We are living proof of this. For some reason, many women put a top priority on personality and a good sense of humor when dating. Most men are a tad more shallow.

9. Men never have to clean a toilet.

Even when I (Rick) lived alone, I called in help for this job. Not a cleaning lady either. I just paid a plumber to come in and change the whole thing— commode, tank, seat, and all. That's so much more sanitary than actually cleaning it. What I'm waiting for is self-cleaning toilets. Why someone hasn't started marketing this is beyond me. We've got self-cleaning ovens, why not self-cleaning toilets?

10. Men can dress faster than women.

Men can be showered and ready to go in ten minutes flat. A woman may take ten minutes just to get a bath ready. She has to pour in the bubble bath, light the candles, get the bath pillow in place, put the CD in the portable CD player, and make sure the water is at the perfect temperature. Then when the phone rings and distracts her for thirty minutes, she has to let the water out and start the process all over again.

This kind of womanly behavior drives me (Rick) crazy on Sunday mornings when I'm trying my best to get the family to church on time. I finally had to tell my wife, Sherri, to please set the alarm earlier, just so she'll be able to get ready before the rest of us ever get up. I love Sherri, but I'm going to have to speak the truth in love on this one. When we're all ready and looking sharp, we'll look around and think, "Hey, we're gonna make it on time this week!" But then the word comes down that Momma hasn't even started getting ready yet, and the collective, "Oh, no," can be heard throughout the entire house.

Ladies, there can't be that much to do to get ready. Why not follow our lead? We men can take a shower, towel dry our hair, throw a little gel in it and we're good to go in a matter of minutes. Having this talent is clearly an advantage for men.

But maybe it's a disadvantage, too. We're the ones who have to wait for you.

ADVANTAGES TO
BEING A WOMAN

No matter what political person is in power, the truth remains: Women rule the world.

THE RICK & BUBBA CODE TO UNDERSTANDING WIFE-SPEAK

Since this book is about secret codes, no code is more secret than the Wife-Speak Code. This ancient tongue, passed down from woman to woman since the dawn of time, is one of the most difficult languages to translate, due to the fact that there are virtually no qualified male translators, and female translators often refuse to cooperate for fear of exposing the code's secrets. This is how wife-speak has managed to keep us guys in the dark for hundreds, even thousands of years.

But take cheer, a small ray of light is now shining through the darkness. After years of research, professors at the Rick and Bubba University of Relational Linguistics in Gadsden, Alabama, are now prepared to break this ancient code and offer to the general public the secret interpretations for the following Wife-Speak phrases:

Wife-speak: *Can you take the kids with you?*

Hidden code: The kids *are* going with you. I don't want to hear your excuses or your whining. These kids have been driving me insane all day and if you don't get them out of here, I may have to start eating my young, beginning with the plumpest and most immature one. That would be you.

Wife-speak: *You're not going to wear that, are you?*

Hidden code: I am completely mortified every time you put that on. You are *not* wearing that. The 80s are over. Save your breath and just go change.

Wife-speak: *We're having a garage sale this Saturday.*

Hidden code: We're having a garage sale this Saturday. Everything that was ever near and dear to you will now be sitting on a table at the end of the driveway bearing a price tag of one nickel. The outfit you were wearing in the previous question, the one that mortifies me every time you put it on, as well as all of your favorite shirts, will be at the top of a stack of clothes priced at $5.00 or best offer. For the entire stack . . . and possibly that lamp your mother gave us. Still safe in the garage will be things that haven't been used one single time throughout our entire marriage, but those items will remain untouched and unsold due to their "collectible" value, or the fact that they hold some sentimental value to me. Only your items will be priced for a "quick sale."

Wife-speak: *Your mom and I were talking and . . .*

Hidden code: It's time to lose weight.

Has also been known to mean: "The worst family vacation of all is coming up. Brace yourself."

Wife-speak: *Let's watch the football game together.*

Hidden code: Record the football game. Record it because you are not going to see a single minute of it. From the moment the center snaps the ball at the beginning of the game, we are going to discuss everything that I've wanted to discuss with you for the last ten years. I am also going to "fake football," which means I'm going to act like I'm all into the game, only I won't be into it at all. And then, just as your team is about to score a touchdown, I am going to make you explain a previous play . . . of a game we watched last season. I also want to know why if there are only two minutes left in the game and your team is already losing by three points, we can't turn it to *Trading Spaces*. Still, the important thing is, we're communicating.

Wife-speak: *We need to talk.*
Hidden code: Unpack. You are *not* going hunting this weekend.

Wife-speak: *Do we have any plans for Saturday?*
Hidden code: You are going to the ballet. Or (even worse), you are going to have dinner with a couple you don't like.
Special Note to Men: This will be one of those situations where your wife likes the wife, but you and the husband don't have a single thing in common. My (Rick) wife tried this on me one day, and two nights later I found myself trying to swallow my steak while a couple of doctors discussed the clamping off of internal organs, new methods of cutting and stitching, and antibiotic-resistant types of discharge. Oh yeah, and how they save people's lives. The only medical thing I could add was, "I can talk like I have helium in my voice."
Further Note to Men: Never once have the words "Do we have any plans for Saturday?" been followed by a wife saying, "Because if we don't, I've got tickets to the football game on the 50-yard line" or "Because I booked you and your buddies a hunting trip." I challenge anyone to find an example throughout the entire history of wife-speak where "Do we have any plans for Saturday?" yielded a positive situation for the husband.

Wife-speak: *Do I look fat in this?*
Hidden code: Where do you want to sleep tonight? If you would like to sleep indoors, a "no" answer is required. The dress can be busting at the seams, but if you're smart and if you enjoy married life, I would strongly

advise you to smile and not say a single word other than *No*.

Note to Betty from Bubba: Honestly, I don't think I've ever seen you look bad in anything you've put on, even at nine months pregnant. Except maybe for that Barney mask. Love, Bubba—(Those who haven't heard the story, please refer to our previous book, *Rick and Bubba's Expert Guide to God, Country, Family, and Anything Else We Can Think Of.*)

P. S. But even in that mask, you still looked pretty good. Rick feels the same way about his wife, Sherri. In fact, I'm sure all you guys feel the same way about your wives, too.

Note to Men: Remember, that question is simply a trick question that women use to trap us. Don't fall for it. Chiropractors' coffers are filled from the bad backs of men who have learned the hard way that the answer to that question may determine whether you end up on the couch for the next month.

THE RICK & BUBBA CODE TO MALE HYGIENE

Male hygiene is one of the reasons why we do not believe in evolution. What ape in his right mind would evolve to a state where he needed to shave and use deodorant every day?

However, as men who like to spend at least part of our time around women, we realize there are certain habits of a hygienic nature that are incumbent upon us. We maintain these duties just to be accepted in society. But along the way, we have discovered a few shortcuts and secrets that we would like to pass on to other men.

Shaving Secrets

Does any man really enjoy shaving? For centuries, we men have stood in front of a bathroom mirror and willingly shed our face and neck blood just so we can appear more attractive to the women we love.

Why? Where did we ever get the idea that this was necessary? The caveman didn't care what he looked or smelled like to his woman. He also had the common sense to know that putting a blade that close to his throat was dangerous.

But not today's man. Not only will we shave hairs delicately close to our carotid arteries, we sometimes do it in the shower with a mirror that keeps fogging up. Again we must ask why. Do we have some kind of latent death wish?

Women shave their legs and under their arms. In the event of a cut, they lose a few drops of blood and go on about their day. We, however, shave our throats. Who devised such a system? Not a man, that's for sure.

Nevertheless, the system is ingrained. So, unless a man wants to be ostracized, join the Taliban, or be a stand-in for ZZ Top, he must comply. The most important thing to know about getting a good shave is to start with a good razor. It used to be that all razors were pretty much the same. They either had a single or a double blade. Today's razors can have fifty blades to get you the closest shave possible. Not only can they shave your beard down to the last standing follicle; they go deep enough to do dental work too.

Electric razors offer variety too. Some vibrate, some have four or more rotaries, and some even come with their own moisturizer for the face. I (Bubba) bought one the other day that came with a built-in cell phone. I had to settle for thatone because the one that picks up satellite radio and sends faxes was backordered.

Speaking of men shaving, do you know that some athletes shave their entire body? Many swimmers, runners, weight-lifters, and other athletes believe that a hairless body gives them a competitive advantage. They also say they appear to have better muscle tone without all that hair covering it up. We agree. You wouldn't believe how toned the two of us are underneath our body hair and three layers of fat. You can't really tell because we don't shave our torsos, but both of us have washboard stomachs. They're just under two loads of lumpy laundry.

Cologne Secrets

I (Rick) am not a cologne guy. The only reason I use cologne is as a signal to my wife. Other than that, I don't wear it. I haven't worn cologne on a regular basis since the eighth grade when I would literally bathe in Brut before heading off to the skating rink. I laid it on so thick you could hardly detect the odor of the rental skates. It was so strong, I'd skate along and the wood flooring would curl up behind me as I went.

These days I don't wear much cologne. Bubba doesn't wear much of it either. He says it makes his nose run. He used to wear a lot of it, though. Back in his Musk days, he went through a bottle a week. He splashed so much of it on him, deer followed him to his car after work. We called his aftershave "Eastern Time Zone" because it always got to the radio station an hour before he did.

A lot of modern colognes have a flowery scent. We don't think this is right. We both believe that men should not smell pretty. If a guy must smell like something, it shouldn't be flowers. It should be the scent of a real man—french fries.

Deodorant Secrets (no pun intended)

With so many deodorants to choose from, it's not easy for a man to find the one he likes. The dry ones feel like rubbing a corncob under your armpit, and the gel ones feel like you're putting jelly under your arms. We don't like the feeling of jelly under our arms.

Once I (Bubba) accidentally used Betty's deodorant. We were on vacation and I had forgotten to bring mine. She uses Secret, so I put some on and thought it would be *my* secret. Lo and behold, I ended up liking it so much, now I buy it for me. I realize they advertise that it's "Strong enough for a man, but made for a woman," but what exactly does that mean? If it's strong enough for us, then I don't see the harm in us using it. Just because it's made for them, should that keep us away?

The interesting thing about this particular deodorant, and it's one reason why I like it, is that it's a gel, but it's measured out. You can't get jelly arm with it. It won't let you. It'll only give you a small amount. I also like it because it smells like my wife and I like having that scent around me at all times. This may be the main reason why I like the deodorant. Rick says my reasoning doesn't compute. If it smells like Betty, then it's going to make me smell like Betty to other people. I can live with that, because it's not a flowery smell. Actually, it smells a little like Old Spice—on me. On Betty it smells more like flowers. How does it do this?

Maybe that's why it's called Secret.

Oral Hygiene

For all you single guys out there—it is a simple fact of life—pork rind breath limits your dating choices. We're not saying it's right. We're just saying you have to accept it.

Fingernails

We realize that there is a growing trend toward men getting manicures. There's nothing wrong with this. It's just not for us. We feel uncomfortable letting someone push back our cuticles, especially when our cuticles may not want to retreat.

Underwear

If the elastic is more stretched out than the national budget, toss it.

THE FATHER'S DAY WARS

We are on a campaign to elevate the status of Father's Day. We are not out to make it better than Mother's Day, only equal. It's long overdue. Dads don't get the same fuss made over them on Father's Day that moms get made over them on Mother's Day. Not even close. We're not whining (okay, maybe a little), but it is a fact.

First, let's look at the typical Father's Day gift. Typical Father's Day gifts are nothing like the typical Mother's Day gift. Moms get flowers, they get taken out to dinner, and sometimes they're given a gift certificate to some luxury spa for a day of pampering. Dads get a tie. More often than not, it's an ugly one . . . that lights up. Again, we don't mean to sound like we're complaining, but let's face it, Father's Day gifts do appear to be an afterthought much of the time.

Heir 1: "It's Father's Day?"

Heir 2: "Did you get him anything?"

Heir 1: "Naw, how 'bout you?"

Heir 2: "Maybe Mom remembered."

Heir 3: "I just talked to her. She forgot too."

Heir 1, or in Rick's case, Heir 4 or 5: "Well, run down to the mini-mart and buy a quart of oil or something before he wakes up. And get me a soda while you're there."

Father's Day is the only gift-giving occasion where it is perfectly acceptable to give someone who doesn't fish a fishing pole, someone who doesn't golf a set of golf balls, a nonsmoker a lighter, and someone who's had a beard for twelve years aftershave.

Another popular "Dad" gift is medical equipment. We don't remember ever asking for a blood pressure monitor, or a cholesterol testing kit, or a year's supply of anti-snoring strips, yet they've been wrapped up and presented to us year after year as though they were tickets to the Super Bowl. And we're supposed to look pleased?

We do, of course. That's because we're good at faking "gift pleasure." We've trained ourselves to show gratitude at even the most insignificant show of appreciation.

"A staple remover! You shouldn't have!"

"Another key chain? That makes twelve now, but *thanks!*"

"More aftershave? Now I can sleep at night knowing I have enough to last me until 2025!"

Mothers, on the other hand, get the royal treatment on their special day. Mother's Day is the number one flower-selling occasion of the entire calendar year. It even beats out Valentine's Day. Obviously, the world knows who it has to answer to—Mom. Moms get better gifts because they've done a good job of scaring the family into submission. If you forget Mom on her day, you know you'll hear about it for the rest of your life . . . and half of your afterlife!

But forget Dad on his day and he'll just take it all in stride. Dads don't want to cause any trouble; their whole existence hangs on not making Mom upset.

Even the advertising agencies tend to overlook dads. For Mother's Day, there will be television commercials that'll rip out your heart with their sentiment. You'll be crying your eyes out as you dial the 800 numbers to order mom all her gifts. For Father's Day, we're lucky if we get a slight mention during a Miracle Ear commercial. Sometimes they'll run an ad that's disguised as a Father's Day gift pitch, but it's really for mom.

It's Father's Day. So, leave those kids with dad and get away for a soothing mineral bath at our luxurious day spa. You deserve it, Mom!

Shoot, Nascar even races on Father's Day, but do you think they'd even dare do that on Mother's Day?

Even the standard issue Father's Day cards don't come to our defense. Mother's Day cards will be all lacey and have page after page of glowing praise for dear ol' Mom. Dad's cards just make fun of how "uncool" we dress (are we really hurting anyone with our black socks and shorts?), or they'll talk about how we embarrass our daughters by insisting we meet the guys they date (even though we barely mentioned the pink hair and didn't say a word about the lip piercings), and they'll talk about how we would fight to the death for our remote controls (even though we . . . okay, they've got us on that one). But they're all laughing "with us" not "at us," right?

The sanctuary is supposed to be immune to society's whims, but we are sad to say that you can even see the Mother's Day-Father's Day inequity in church. On Mother's Day, all the moms are given a rose as soon as they enter the sanctuary. Every song in the music program will be geared toward honoring Mom. They will ask the youngest mom, the oldest, and the mother with the most children to stand and receive the applause due them. Mothers will be heralded in the pastor's sermon as very possibly the closest thing to the Godhead. Not a negative word is spoken against mothers the entire service.

On Father's Day, it's a different story. Dads walk in, and they're handed a pencil with "Happy Father's Day" engraved on it—but it's misspelled. (Does it say Happy Fat he's day on purpose?) After the soloist opens with "Cat's in the Cradle," the sermon will be anything from, "Deadbeat Dads" to "At Least Your Heavenly Father is Perfect." Key points of the lesson will likely be something like this: If families are in disarray, it's Dad's fault. If the kids are spoiled, it's Dad's fault. If they're denied, it's Dad's fault. If mom's unhappy, it's Dad's fault. If the stock market plunges, it's Dad's fault. If there's global warming, it's Dad's fault.

A pastor would never go after moms like this on Mother's day. "Why?" you ask.

He's scared of her, too.

(By the way, another thing we've never been able to understand about our society is this: if a mom stays home to take care of the kids, in many circles she's considered a hero. If a dad stays home to take care of these same kids, he's often considered a loser. That just doesn't seem fair. Where are the Father's Day cards for stay-at-home dads?)

It's just our opinion, but we feel that Dad has gotten the short end of the respect stick long enough now and that's why we're on a campaign to change all that. Again, we're not seeking to diminish Mother's Day in any way. We both have mothers—and we're afraid of them, too. But it's high time that our nation raised the level of Father's Day up a notch or two. That's all we're saying. Skip the tie this year, and get Dad a four-wheeler! That'd put the "Happy" back in Father's Day! And while we're at it, get Hollywood to give us some television shows and movies that show us dads in a positive light. That'd be a great gift, too.

Now more than ever the world needs dads who are shown respect. Where's the Father who Knows Best? Or Beaver's dad? Or Andy Griffith? And come to think of it, where's that quart of oil from the mini-mart? And how'd you know that's exactly what we wanted? *Thanks!*

THE RICK & BUBBA CODE FOR DETERMINING YOUR "GUY QUOTIENT"

After countless interviews and endless research, we have condensed all of our findings from locker rooms, deer woods, and race tracks all across America into one simple quiz for determining "guy quotient":

1. If your wife seems to be having a particularly bad hair day, do you

   a) Recognize her need for reassurance, take her in your arms, and once again pledge your undying love.
   b) Recognize her need for support and ask if there is anything at all that you can do to help ease her load.
   c) Hide out in the garage until the coast is clear.

2. When your wife is walking into the house carrying several bags of groceries, do you

   a) Jump up out of the recliner and take the bags from her arms, asking if there are any more groceries in the car that you could help her with.

b) Tell her you'll get the groceries later, then offer to give her a neck and foot massage.

c) Ask if she remembered the batteries for the remote control and tell her to shut the door to get the glare off the television screen.

3. The correct way to replace a roll of toilet paper is

a) On the holder in the "over" position.

b) On the holder in the "under" position.

c) Replace it?

4. Complete this sentence: A funeral is a good time to

a) Remember the life of the deceased and console his or her surviving loved ones with warm and caring memories. And maybe send a casserole.

b) Reflect on the shortness of life. And maybe eat a casserole.

c) Tell jokes to the guy standing next to you.

5. You've been seeing a woman for several years. She's attractive, funny, and intelligent; and you always enjoy being with her. One leisurely Sunday afternoon, the two of you are taking it easy. You're watching the football game. She's reading the paper. Could life get any better than this? Then suddenly out of the clear blue she tells you that she thinks she has really fallen for you, but she can no longer bear the uncertainty of not knowing where the relationship is going. She's not asking whether you want to settle down and get married—only if you believe that you have some kind of future together. She just desperately wants some sign of commitment from you. What should you say?

a) That you sincerely think the two of you have a future together but you don't want to rush it. After all, you've only been dating twelve years.

b) You have strong feelings for her but you cannot honestly say that you'll be ready to settle down anytime soon and you don't want to give her false hope. After all, you've only been dating twelve years.

c) You cannot believe the Jets called a draw play on 3rd and 17.

6. You have met the woman of your dreams and you want to spend the rest of your life with her—sharing all the joys and sorrows, triumphs and tragedies, adventures and opportunities that this world has to offer, come what may. How do you tell her?

a) You take her to a nice restaurant (even go inside this time) and open your heart to her after dinner.
b) You take her for a stroll on a moonlit beach and tell her of your decision under the stars.
c) You tell her what?

7. One weekday morning your wife wakes up feeling ill and asks you to pack the school lunches for your three children. Your first question to her is

a) Which one's the vegetarian?
b) Can't they just buy a hot lunch at school?
c) There are three of them?

8. The only time that it is acceptable to toss out a set of veteran underwear is

a) When it has developed holes so large that you're not sure which ones were originally intended for your legs to go through.
b) When it is down to eight loosely connected underwear molecules, hanging together so slightly that it has to be handled with tweezers.
c) There is never an acceptable time to throw away veteran underwear. In fact, you check the garbage regularly in case *someone* (you're not naming names here but the someone looks an awful

lot like your wife) is quietly trying to discard a pair of underwear she is frankly jealous of because you've known it longer than you've known her.

9. What, in your opinion, was the most reasonable explanation for the fact that Moses led the Israelites in circles all over the desert before they got to the Promised Land?

a) He was being tested.
b) He wanted them to appreciate the Promised Land when they got there.
c) Like any red-blooded man, he didn't need to ask directions because he was "sure it was just around the next corner."

10. What is the human race's single greatest achievement?

a) Democracy
b) Landing a man on the moon
c) The remote control

Every time you answered *c*, give yourself a point. If you scored 10, you are definitely a real guy. If you scored more than 10, you're not very good at math.

OPINION-LESS

Neither one of us take opinion polls any more. Like many married men, we left our opinions at the altar. Not all of our opinions, of course. When it comes to politics, the direction of our country, the kinds of foods that we like, and the people that irritate us, we are still very much opinionated.

But certain opinions of ours have, for all practical purposes, vanished. One of the areas where we no longer have an opinion is in the arena of home improvements. We used to have opinions about that, but like we said, they reside in that pile of opinions we left at the altar.

Don't get us wrong. We're not wimps. We just don't care enough about those opinions to go back to the chapel and pick them up. It's probably closed anyway. Besides, marriage manuals will tell you to choose your battles and we've chosen. House improvements just aren't worth the fight.

To all of you married guys reading this book who might disagree with that last sentence, we want you to know that, like you, we too have watched our share of the home redecorating shows. We too have been forced to look at paint samples and upholstery swatches against our wills. And, like a television game show, a buzzer would sound if we dared to select the one that was not our wife's favorite, and we would be told to pick again.

So we would.

BUZZZZZZZ! Wrong again. The buzzer would continue sounding

until all choices other than our wife's choice were eliminated. This entire process took place to the tune of repeated assurances that our "opinion really does matter."

But let's get real. If our opinions mattered, we would see more model homes that looked like a man lived there. When's the last time you went on a Parade of Homes tour and saw a deer head hanging on a wall? Or a 7-foot stuffed marlin displayed over the sofa? Or a refrigerator for cold drinks next to the recliner? Exactly. We rest our case. When it comes to home decorating, the man's opinion really doesn't matter. If it did, would we ever have had sofas with so many pillows that you're left with only three inches of seating space? No man worth his salt would have ever suggested that. If a man's opinion mattered, here is what the perfect home would look like:

1. There would be no curtains throughout the entire house. Why cover up a view that you just paid $20,000 extra for? Why even have windows if all we're going to do is cover them up with fabric? It doesn't make sense.

2. There would be no china cabinet in the house because china would not be allowed on the premises. Men do not understand the concept of buying a $2,000 china cabinet to hold $500 worth of china that no one ever eats off of. Paper plates only cost around two bucks, and you don't need a china cabinet to keep the dust off them. They come with their own plastic bag. And don't even get us started on the china plates that get hung on a wall. Plates aren't a decoration. They're kitchenware. You don't see a pair of barbeque tongs hanging on the wall trying to pass itself off as a work of art. Barbeque tongs know their place. Plates should too.

3. Deer heads would serve as towel and clothes hangers. They're perfect. The larger ones could be used as coat racks. If you ever need more hangers, it would be a good excuse to go hunting again.

4. Every room in the house would have a lounge chair. Nothing else. Just a lounge chair. That's really all you need in a room. Okay, maybe a couple of TV trays and a big-screen television set. But that's it, except

in the bedrooms. They would need a bed, too. A bed, a lounge chair, a couple of TV trays and a big-screen TV. Basic-needs decorating. Where's the HGTV show for that?

5. To men, a furniture purchase is for life. We're loyal. There will be none of this tossing a piece of furniture aside just because next year's model looks prettier. Men aren't that fickle. We just cannot grasp how a piece of furniture that our wives "couldn't live without" in 1994 is suddenly a Goodwill discard thirteen short years later.

6. The only pictures hanging on the walls would be of the wife and kids. Why would we have a painting of fruit on our walls? If we want to see fruit, we can look in the fridge!

7. There would be no live plants whatsoever in the house. When mankind came indoors, weren't we done with living around plants? If we want to live in the rainforest, we'll get our shots and fly there. We don't want to have to get malaria shots just to walk through our living rooms.

8. Each family member would be given one towel. The color does not matter. It's their towel and they are responsible for it for the remainder of their lives. After bathing they are to simply dry off and then hang their towel over the shower door (or on one of the deer heads) and use it the next time. There would be no such thing as a guest towel. It's unsanitary for a string of visitors to the house to be using the same towel. Guests who want to dry their hands, provided they've actually washed them, can do what we do whenever we're guests in their homes—use the furniture.

9. Positively no scented candles. What genius decided we men wanted our houses to smell like vanilla or pumpkins? If we want our homes to have that kind of aroma, our wives can just bake a pie. Or we can buy one at the store and bring it home. Or even attempt to make one ourselves. We don't want to smell pumpkin pie and then not be able to get a slice of it. In this country, that's what we call cruel and unusual punishment.

10. Last but not least, if men were designing the house, dining rooms would not exist. Why have a room just to "pretend" that you eat in there? Everyone knows that nobody ever really eats in a dining room, so why go on with the cherade? Get rid of the room altogether. Or if you must keep it, put something in there that you'll really use—like a pool table . . . and a deer head to hold the cue sticks.

PART II

DECODING ROMANCE

You may not have realized this, but we would never have earned the title of the "Two Sexiest Fat Men Alive" unless we were known to have a certain way with the ladies. By ladies, we mean our wives, Betty and Sherri. And though we have made our share of mistakes, along the way we have learned much in the ways of romance and intrigue.

So read on, Romeo and Juliet. You may learn a thing or two.

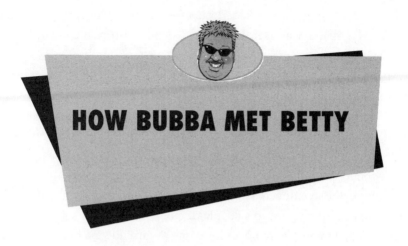

HOW BUBBA MET BETTY

Probably one of the greatest mysteries known to man is how Betty and I ever became husband and wife. We've been married now for almost twenty years, but if you had been standing off to the side watching our lives way back when, looking at how our paths crossed, crisscrossed, and then crossed again, you might have wondered if we were ever going to end up together at all. We didn't have the paparazzi following us around like Tom Cruise and Katie Holmes, but on the surface it sure seemed like *Mission Impossible*.

Here's how it all happened:

I was attending Jacksonville High School. There were only two high schools in our community: Jacksonville (the larger school) and Pleasant Valley (the smaller but newer one). A friend of mine was dating a girl from Pleasant Valley. This Pleasant Valley girl started thinking that if she could match me up with someone from her school, then I would want to hang out there more and bring her boyfriend with me. That, she figured, would be a win-win situation for all of us! I was unaware of her plan, but one night at one of the various athletic events at her school, she told me to pick out any girl I saw and she would match me up with her.

"What about her?" I said, pointing to one of the cheerleaders.

"Except her," she said. "She's been in love with the same guy since the first grade. Pick someone else."

I looked down the line of cheerleaders and picked the bouncy blonde at the end. Her name was Betty, and my friend's girlfriend nodded, then immediately went to work at trying to match us up.

My next encounter with the lovely Betty was at a beauty pageant where she was competing. I had come from an eye appointment where I had gotten my eyes dilated, so for a short while I thought she was twins. She looked great, though, even through dilated eyes. And as my eyes grew more focused, my interest in Betty grew even stronger. (Betty must have looked pretty good to the judges too because she won first runner-up.)

Through the continued encouragement of her matchmaking friend, Betty ended up inviting me to a couple of other events at her school, including an athletic banquet. I've never been one to turn down a banquet, and as many of you know I do love sports, so I was really looking forward to going. But before I could leave, I had to cut the grass for my parents. We had a big yard, and all I had to cut it with was one of those push-mowers. I did it, but afterwards, I was exhausted. I lay down to take a little nap and ended up falling dead asleep. I didn't wake up until ten o'clock that night! My heart sank when I realized that I had just unintentionally stood up this beautiful girl that I really was starting to care about. Would she ever take my call again? Would she let me tell her how sorry I was? Could she ever forgive me?

Yes. And no. Betty took the call, but she didn't buy the excuse. She was understandably upset and wouldn't accept the fact that I had unintentionally overslept.

I defended myself to myself. (I was the only one listening.) After all, it was a big yard. But I decided not to push my luck anymore with Betty. Until college, that is; that's when I happened to run into her again. It was at a blood donor drive. (Let's see Tom Cruise top that one. Anyone can woo a girl in Italy. It takes a real man to make a blood donor drive romantic.)

Standing there by the bags of B positive and O negative, we chatted for a while. Betty says now that I asked her for the cookie they gave her, but I don't think that's true. I do remember the distinct taste of chocolate chips in my mouth as we were talking, but I was probably imagining it. It was so long ago that the details are blurry. Things got a little blurry for Betty back then, too, because after donating blood Betty got terribly dizzy and fainted right there in front of me! (Honest, I don't think I ate her cookie. And even if I did, she probably would have fainted anyway. It wasn't that big of a cookie.)

I thought about giving her mouth to mouth resuscitation, just in case she needed it. That's the kind of Good Samaritan I am. But the nurse rushed over and brought Betty back to consciousness by just fanning her awake.

"Sugar," she said, helping her to her feet. "We've got to get you up off the floor. You're bad for business."

See, we were all looking out for Betty's best interests. Over the years, I've often teased Betty that it was at that moment, there on the floor of that blood donor center that she really fell for me. But in reality, I still hadn't won the sweet Betty Lou over, and I wouldn't for some time yet.

Five or six more years to be exact. But then one day, the radio station I was working for was doing a remote at a video store and who did I happen to run into there but Betty. I asked her how she'd been, thinking that maybe we could pick up where we left off. But she told me that she was engaged. An engagement can really put a damper on the whole flirting game. So I congratulated her—not very enthusiastically, but I did congratulate her. Then she handed me a piece of paper with her phone number on it and told me to call her.

Call her? Whoa . . . had I heard her right? Betty wanted me to call her? She was engaged. And I was the guy who stood her up, then allegedly ate her cookie and caused her to pass out at the blood donor bank. Why would she be handing me her phone number now, especially since she had just told me that she was engaged? But it was true. I was holding what appeared to be a legitimate telephone number. It had seven digits.

Needless to say, it wasn't long before I gave the lovely Betty a call. And yes, it was a legitimate number all right. It just wasn't hers. Betty had given me a bogus number. At that moment, that beautiful girl was surely at home laughing about how she finally got the ultimate revenge on the boy who had stood her up.

But two weeks later, Betty got in touch with me and asked me why I hadn't called her. I told her what I was sure she already knew, that it was a wrong number. Betty laughed and explained that she must have given me the wrong number by mistake. She sounded sincere, but it still smelled a little too much like revenge to me. To convince me of her true intentions, Betty suggested we go see a movie together. I agreed to go, but I just knew that Betty had lined up some big country boys to beat me to a pulp just as I arrived at her house to pick her up. So I formed a back-up plan just in case. I told her that since I didn't know where she lived, we could meet up at the local McDonald's instead. I figured no one with any shred of decency would beat a guy to a pulp in front of a clown.

So we met up at McDonald's. Betty got into my car, and from there we went to the show. Afterward, I brought her back to her car at McDonald's. By then, I had relaxed and decided that it hadn't been a setup at all. Feeling good about that, I told her before leaving that night, "Hey, I'm going to marry you." (She had passed the most important test for marriage. No hit men.)

I really wasn't sure what Betty's feelings were for me. They must have been somewhat significant because after that date, she broke off her engagement with the other guy.

But our romance was to have its own ups and downs. After dating quite steadily for some time, and thinking that things were going good, one day Betty told me that she wanted to break up. She thought we were moving too quickly into a relationship. I tried to be understanding, but I didn't want to break up. Didn't I have a vote in this? I said, "It takes two people to date, and it takes two people to break up. I'll see you tomorrow."

Now, don't get me wrong. I'm all for the Nineteenth Amendment. I know Betty had a right to vote in the matter and I wanted to respect her decision. But our paths had crossed too many times to just go our separate ways. I knew Betty and I were meant to be together. I told myself that I was going to hang in there until Betty was convinced of it, too. No matter what she did, I was going to be open to keeping the relationship alive. If this happened with today's laws, they might consider it borderline stalking. It wasn't. It was just one party refusing to stop believing, waiting patiently until the relationship became just as important to the other party. If more couples did this, maybe the divorce rate in this country would finally start to drop.

In my situation, my patience paid off. As of the writing of this book, Betty and I have been happily married seventeen years and have two beautiful children. And no, I haven't stood her up since. But I have been known to swipe a few of her chocolate chip cookies.

HOW RICK MET SHERRI

Actually, this chapter should be called The Rick and Bubba Code of Marrying Up. Anyone can marry down. But as Bubba and I both know it takes ingenuity, talent, and determination to marry up. Believe me, this is a practice that we highly recommend. Every man should honestly believe in his heart that he married up. It keeps you grateful, keeps your pride in check, and reminds you on a daily basis that you would be lost without your "better half." Bubba and I know this beyond any shadow of a doubt. If Bubba and I ever forget, our fans and any recent family photo will remind us of it.

I met Sherri when I was doing a solo radio show. Bubba was an engineer at that station and had gotten me the job. To mix things up a bit, I had Bubba join me on the air from time to time. Being old college buddies, our humor already worked well together and we had a lot of fun on the air, but *The Rick and Bubba Show* was yet to be birthed.

A young lady by the name of Sherri Bodine had just been hired as the new newsgirl at the station. I had heard about this new girl, but we hadn't met yet, until one day I saw her walking down the hallway at work. You remember Roy Orbison's song, "Pretty Woman"? That's exactly what played in my mind. I remember saying to myself, *That is the most beauti-*

ful woman I have ever seen. It didn't occur to me that this beautiful woman was probably not thinking, *That's the most handsome man that I have ever seen.* The song going through her head was probably more like "Walk On By."

Here I was, six years older than she was, with a mullet (a hairstyle that I'd hung onto a lot longer than I should have; but as mullets go, it did look pretty good). And I had kids. I soon discovered that Sherri had something too—a boyfriend. I honored those boundaries and didn't ask her out until her boyfriend moved away to Florida and word got around the station that they had broken up. I figured someone had to be there to help her get through it, and I was ready to volunteer.

Okay, not quite ready. It wasn't until that December that I finally got the courage to ask Sherri out. Since she had planned to spend Christmas with her family and I was going to be spending it with my kids, Boomer and Jo Jo, we decided that we would wait until after the holidays to plan our first date.

But by then, Sherri was having cold feet. When we both came back to work, Sherri didn't want to talk about dating. She wanted to talk about not dating. She said that she had been thinking about it and had decided that we should just "be friends."

Now, before I go on, I just want to say something to you girls out there. You need a heads up on this one fact about men. If you're single, and especially if you're pretty, no guy wants to just be your "pal." He may be a great listener, a shoulder to cry on when your other boyfriends dump you; but down deep, he wants to date you himself. He may not even realize this, or even act on it should the opportunity arise, but this will be his underlying feeling at all times. He will be constantly thinking, "I could date you."

I wasn't interested in having Sherri Bodine as "just a friend." I had enough friends and I told her so. Overweight, funny guys get cast in the "friend" role all the time and far too quickly. I wanted to one day be Sherri's husband. If all she wanted was a new friend, I was ready to move on.

And I did.

Never one to miss a good radio campaign, however, I started telling our listeners that I was going to marry Sherri Bodine. I even played a parody of "Wonderful Tonight" by Eric Clapton that I had written for her. I don't remember the exact words, but my version was, "Read Me the News Tonight."

Fans of the show got in on the fun and would call in trying to convince Sherri to give me a chance. Some listeners told her to run as far away from me as she could. (But I didn't let my family call in that often.) Thankfully, the vast majority of the call-ins were from people telling Sherri to "give the guy a break."

Still, she wouldn't budge. And like I said, I had moved on.

Another way I dealt with Sherri's rejection (all right, I hadn't totally moved on) was to start looking for flaws in her. I figured if I could find enough flaws, then I would be glad that I was never going to be married to her.

I couldn't deny the fact that she was pretty, so I had to convince myself that she had all sorts of hidden flaws. One of those flaws had to have been her legs. I had never even caught a glimpse of them before (she always wore jeans or pants to the station), so I told myself that there had to be something wrong with her legs, and that's why she was hiding them. But then one day she wore a dress to work and blew that theory right out of the water.

No matter how hard I tried, I couldn't find anything wrong with Sherri Bodine, except for the fact that she only wanted to be my friend.

One night, though, while we were doing a remote broadcast, Sherri came over to me and said something that I couldn't quite hear. Sherri's only five feet tall (bless her heart, she probably thinks she's five-feet-one), so I leaned down to get closer to her mouth so I could hear what she was saying.

I don't know what came over me at that moment, but with her lips in such close range, the temptation was just too great. I didn't sense Sherri putting up any roadblocks either. So I pressed my lips to hers and kissed her. It was just a little kiss, but I had done it. I had given it one final shot, and to my grateful surprise she kissed me back!

Lesson learned? Sometimes it's good to be bold, to let the other person know how you truly feel instead of going around playing all these mind games and losing out on so much of life. It's risky to be vulnerable. To risk rejection. But I'm glad I risked it. I'm glad I didn't give up on Sherri and our relationship. I'm glad I didn't push her, but hung in there long enough for her feelings for me to change. I'm glad Sherri Bodine no longer wanted us to "just be friends."

From that moment on, neither one of us ever dated anyone else. We knew we were meant to be together. And today, after eleven years of marriage and three kids (along with the two children I came with, making a total of five), Sherri still looks as good to me now as she did then.

I don't know if you saw the report that came out recently that said that men are actually smarter than women, but I tend to agree with this assessment and I'll illustrate why. Bubba and I were joking around about this on the show one morning, and afterward someone at the station challenged me on it.

"Women are a lot smarter than men!" she said, correcting me.

"You think so?" I said.

"Absolutely!"

"Well, men are smarter and I'll prove it," I said. "Look at me and Sherri the next time we're walking down the hallway and you tell me which one you think is smarter."

She didn't say another word.

It's settled.

VALENTINE ANXIETY

If it wasn't for Valentine's Day, psychologists all across America would be driving much smaller cars. Many of us still bear battle scars from childhood celebrations of this unpredictable and potentially devastating holiday. Cupid may look innocent, but those are real arrows he's packing, and for every bull's-eye he hits, there are a hundred misfires. Often straight into vital organs.

On the surface, Valentine's Day sounds like a good idea. Even we'll admit that. A day dedicated to love, chocolate, and overpriced flowers— what could possibly be wrong with something like that?

Nothing, unless you're a third grader and an empty Valentine bag sends you into intensive therapy for the greater portion of your adult life.

Let's face it, Valentine's is a make-or-break day. Unlike the Fourth of July (where your self-esteem stays intact even if you don't win the three-legged race), and Christmas (where even if you don't get the toy you wanted, you can usually convince yourself that you're still loved), Valentine's Day plays havoc with your self-worth in a way that should have been classified illegal years ago.

I (Rick) have had just enough therapy to be able to talk about my string of Valentine's Day disasters. In elementary school, I was a chubby kid. I wasn't any thinner or better looking when Valentine's Day rolled around either. Valentine's Day was the day when I tended to take life, love, and a box of 99-cent Valentine's Day cards just a little too seriously. If a girl gave me a card with the Disney character Goofy on it, and the printing on the card said, "I'm Goofy for you," I thought she really meant that. All the way home after school I'd be thinking to myself, *Emily Johnson is goofy for me! It says it right there on the card, she's goofy for me. That's gotta mean she's goofy for me!*

I was pathetic.

But it wasn't all my fault. Valentine's Day held unbelievable anxiety for a lot of us kids back then. The way schools did Valentine's Day was set up for disaster. Students had to sit in their seats holding their breath as the teacher dismissed each row one at a time to get up and go pass out their cards. Since your eyes were closed, you never knew who was going to get a card and whose bag was going to be passed over. Talk about a defining moment to set up your ability, or inability, to handle rejection the rest of your life. The sweat would start beading up on your little forehead, and your heart pounded as row after row delivered those all-important envelopes. (This is also when you first learned to pray in school.) You would be happy even if that snotty girl who'd annoyed you in class all semester gave you a card. Or your teacher. Or the school lunch lady. You just didn't want an empty bag.

I'm surprised there hasn't been a Valentine's Day psycho tracking down every second grade classmate who didn't leave him or her a Valentine's Day card. We never would do anything like that, of course, but we do have our list.

Things have changed, though. These days, most teachers do their best to shield boys and girls from the kind of emotional trauma that an empty Valentine's bag can cause. Children are instructed to bring enough valentines for the entire class, ensuring a "no child left behind" policy. That doesn't help our generation, but at least it'll prevent future Valentine's Day damage to young minds and hearts.

I (Bubba) remember one particular Day of the Cupid that had all the potential of sentencing me to years of Prozac. At least that's the way it started out. I remember it like it was yesterday. I was in Mrs. Wright's class. Great little place it was. Each of us had made our Valentine bags, printed our names on them in block letters, and then placed them on the shelf at the back of the room. I sat breathless with my eyes closed tightly as the other classes came in and took their turn passing out their cards. I couldn't wait for them to be done so I could go check my bag and see who gave me a card. The big jackpot was if you got one of those cards with those little heart candies inside. The ones that said, "Be mine!" "Kiss me" or "If you ever donate blood, can I eat your cookie?"

I know now, of course, that if my bag had been empty that day, there could have been many other reasons for it. It could have been because I was shy and didn't know very many of the other kids. It could have been because when the students walked by with their cards, they couldn't read the way I had written my name on the bag, and so they passed on by. It could have even been that since the bags were so close together, someone else got the cards that were intended for me. An empty bag did not automatically mean that I was the most hated child on the campus. I know that now. But back then that's the way an empty Valentine's bag made you feel. Rejected. Passed over. Tossed aside. Basically, the way Rick and I used to feel during ratings season.

(Thankfully those feelings are behind us now. Thankfully, the radio show continues to climb in the ratings, and our wives are bound by the marriage contract to give us annual Valentine's Day cards. We've also had years to process the pain, so we can cope with these sorts of things better.)

So there I was sitting in Mrs. Wright's class waiting for messages from Cupid. Mrs. Young's class came downstairs, and of course, my "girlfriend" was in Mrs. Young's class. We could hear them just outside the door, and my heart began to race.

Now I should explain before I go on that my "girlfriend" wasn't really my girlfriend. When you're in first, second, or third grade, all you have is an "almost girlfriend." A grade school "almost" girlfriend is a lot different than a high school or college girlfriend. High school or college girlfriends are someone you usually spend hours talking to. In first grade, you NEVER EVER EVER talk to your girlfriend. You admire her from afar, you might even daydream about her, but you don't dare speak to her. You avoid her at all costs. To do anything else would be a major social taboo.

Mrs. Young's class came in and after we were told to close our eyes, they began passing out their cards. My palms were sweating, my heart was about ready to pound itself out of my chest, and I knew all of my hopes were about to be realized or smashed to smithereens.

I desperately wanted to, but I resisted peeking to see who was putting something in my bag. I just sat there with my eyes closed while every emotion in my little body lay open and vulnerable. Can any of you relate to this? Are you feeling my anxiety? I'm nervous and sweating just writing about it.

What added to my anticipation was the fact that word had already been going around the playground that I was going to get a lock of hair in my Valentine's Day card. A LOCK OF HAIR! That was way better than a Goofy card, even better than those little heart candies. A lock of hair was the ultimate Valentine card attachment for any elementary schoolboy!

After Mrs. Young's class was through passing out their valentines, I opened my eyes and looked down the line of students until I saw her. Susan was her name. I sat there, staring at her like Mowgli from the Jungle Book, hypnotized by her beauty. I won't say Susan's last name, but she knows who she is. She is a nurse now, just like my beautiful wife, Betty Lou. Funny how you're drawn to certain personality types, even from childhood.

After I pulled myself out of my trance, I looked to the back of the room at my bag. There was this huge envelope sticking out of it. I mean HUGE! It was so big it was about to topple the whole bag over. When the other kids in the class saw it, they started whooping and hollering. They knew I had hit pay dirt. I knew I had hit pay dirt. This was the best Valentine's Day of my life! (Up to that point of my life, that is.) The day was unfolding just as I had imagined it.

With my heart pounding I walked over to my bag and opened her card, and sure enough, there was one of those golden locks of hair taped inside that card. The entire rest of the day I was walking on air! When they served orange juice and crackers that day, I said, "Give me a double!" I didn't care how much homework our teacher gave us that night. Or the rest of the week, for that matter. In fact, that Valentine's Day made my fourth, fifth, and sixth grade years just sail right on by.

I've had a thing for blondes ever since. That may be one of the reasons I was attracted to Betty Lou. It was that golden hair. It's a weakness with me, I guess.

I have to confess that in a deep, dark hideaway spot, that card and that lock of hair still exist. Betty Lou knows about this and she's fine with it. She knows it was just a childhood crush. Susan and I never ended up dating when we got older. We just grew up and went our separate ways. But I've got to tell you that I get that same rush whenever Betty Lou gives me a Valentine's Day card. My mind can't help but go back to that day in elementary school when everything I had hoped for came to pass. The card was there, the lock of hair was there, and my self-esteem soared.

And not to be outdone, over the years I've been given a few locks of Betty Lou's hair too.

WHATEVER

I have a hair story too. But mine didn't go quite as well as Bubba's. Now, I admit I wasn't really listening that day. I saw Sherri's lips moving, and I knew something audible was coming out of her mouth, but my mind was elsewhere. Looking back now, I do think I heard her say that she was going to get her hair done, maybe even try something a little different. But I wouldn't bet the Big Boy statue at the radio station on it. The only thing I can say for certain is that I remember seeing her lips moving after which I answered her with a loving, "Yeah, yeah, whatever." That is where the problem appears to have first developed.

History bears out that whatever happens after a husbandly "Whatever" is clearly the husband's own fault.

Allow me to prove my case . . .

Eve: "I'm going for a walk to the forbidden tree, honey. Want me to bring you back anything?"
Adam: "Whatever."

Custer's wife: "I don't feel good about this Little Big Horn trip, George. Are you sure you should go?"
Custer: "Whatever."

Mary Todd Lincoln: "We can go to the football game or we can go to a play. But I'd really like to see this play."
Abraham: "Whatever."

Hillary Clinton: "Hey, that new intern my friend recommended is starting today."
Bill: "Whatever."

See, guys, those "whatever" answers will get us every time. But on this particular day, the dilemma I found myself in after my "whatever" answer wasn't your usual run-of-the-mill Rick Burgess mess-up. This one had the potential for dire consequences. I didn't see any of it coming, and finding my way out was going to be like walking through a minefield.

All I really knew beyond any doubt was that Sherri had said something to me about hair—or it might have been the fair?—and then walked out the door. I also remember saying "Whatever," but now that she had been gone for several hours, I was starting to get a little concerned. I had no clue exactly where she was or what she was doing.

Just when I started to wonder if I should set up the search and rescue team, my phone rang. It was Sherri calling from her cell phone.

She told me that she was at the beauty salon and needed to talk to me. She was alive and reporting in, so I thought, well, that's a good thing. So far I was doing fine in the minefield so I breathed a sigh of relief.

"I'm thinking about not doing highlights this time," she said, as if I understood what in the world highlights were. "I've been looking at Big Love's hair, and I kind of like his golden color. That's really my natural color, you know. More of a honey blonde."

Big Love is our son and he has beautiful gold, honey blonde hair. I thought to myself, well, it's all still blonde. That wouldn't be that much of a change. So what's the big deal and why is she calling to ask me about it?

Again, totally focused on the situation, I said, "Well, whatever. Just don't cut it short."

Did you catch the "whatever"? This was my second *whatever* in a 24-hour period. I wasn't just walking through a minefield. I was breakdancing my way through it. I should have been paying way more attention, but for *whatever* reason my mind had gone AWOL.

Later that day when I got home from work, my mind still wasn't anywhere near where it should have been. All I could think of was rushing downstairs to my office. Sherri's mother was in town and could watch Taz; Big Love was at preschool, and the setting was perfect for me to finally spend some quality work time getting my office space organized in our new house.

But the best-laid plans of mice and radio show hosts are soon interrupted by reality. Mine came in the form of another call from Sherri. I could tell by the hysterical sobs in my ear that she was upset about something.

I did a quick run-through of my inner calendar. Anniversary? No. Birthday? No. Have I said anything stupid? Nothing out of the ordinary. Feeling reasonably safe, I asked,

"What's wrong, honey?"

"Oh, I'm ffff-fine," she said, her voice cracking.

"No, you're not. What's wrong?"

"Rick, you're going to hate my hair!"

Now, someone bullying my wife, I can handle. Someone teasing her, I'll put an end to it in no time flat. Someone talking about her behind her back, they'll be toast by the time I'm through with them. But a hair crisis? This sort of thing is clearly out of a husband's area of expertise. This sort of thing is what girlfriends were created for.

But Sherri didn't call her girlfriend. She called me.

"They said they had to turn it all one color before they could put the new color on," she said, trying her best to get the words out between sobs.

Turn it all one color? Wasn't it already one color? She might as well have started talking in Farsi. I had no clue what she was talking about. None of it sounded like anything that would make a person cry. I'd still love my wife if they colored all of her hair, part of it, or none of it. So in my understanding way, I tried to cheer her up the best I could. "Hey, are you ugly?" I said. "Are you so different, I won't recognize you? Just bring your I.D. when you come home."

It wasn't Dr. Phil, but it was the best I could do under the circumstances.

We talked a little more, but she was still pretty upset. We hung up, and all I could do was wait. Sometimes that's the only thing you can do in a mine-field—stay put and don't take another step.

It wasn't long before I heard her coming in the front door. I called up from the basement and asked if she wanted me to come upstairs.

"No!" she hinted, loud enough for the neighbors to hear.

I knew it was important to honor her wishes, to give her some space, to let her ease her way into her new look. She would get used to it eventually. After all, how bad could it be? And even if she absolutely hated it, she could color it again, or even shave it all off and start over. Either way, it wasn't the end of the world. And absolutely not the end of our marriage. I still loved her, I knew that. *Whatever* her hair looked like.

I knew, however, that eventually I was going to have to come upstairs. Sherri couldn't hide from me forever. At some point, I would have to rejoin the family. I couldn't spend the rest of my life holed up in the basement. I had to return to the main part of the house and help run our family. There would be graduations, weddings, grandchildren. I couldn't miss all of that. Sooner or later, I was going to have to come upstairs and see what they had done to her hair.

I decided that it might as well be sooner. Sherri was just going to have to accept that fact. After a brief pause, I started up the stairs, mentally preparing myself for what might be awaiting me. I was picturing every hor-rible thing that could have happened to her hair. But none of them were so bad that it would change my feelings for her. When I said for better or for worse I meant it.

When I reached the top of the stairs, Sherri came out of the room and just stood there. My mouth fell open. I was speechless. True, I had vowed my unwavering love. But I wasn't prepared for this. I am not exaggerating, my wife looked amazing! Her hair was a totally different color, but it looked fantastic! Breathtaking! I couldn't get over it! All these years I had been married to a beautiful blonde, and now I was married to a gorgeous redhead!

I started telling her how terrific she looked, but from the look on her face I soon realized that not only was I breakdancing through this mine-field, I had now started playing frisbee in it. I was making so much of a fuss over her new look that Sherri started getting jealous . . . of herself!

"Well, you're just really fired up about this, aren't you?" she said.

"No, no, you're taking this all wrong," I said. "I'm just telling you that I like this new look. It's really sexy. That's all. You're my wife. I can compliment my wife, can't I?"

"So you're saying I wasn't sexy before?" she snapped.

Without knowing it, I had landed knee-deep in the "Do I look fat in this dress" quagmire. It would have been nice if someone had bumped up the security alert chart a couple of colors, but they didn't. I had no warning.

Sherri continued with her interrogation. "What are you saying? Are you saying I was some 'ug' walking around before?"

"Of course not, honey."

"You've always hated my blonde hair, haven't you? You've always preferred redheads."

"Look, all I'm saying is you look great. I got two words for you: Angie Everhorn. Remember that model who had that auburn/chestnut kind of hair? That's who you look like."

Bad move. The Angie Everhorn reference only made her think that I'd been married to her all these years while secretly wishing she was Angie Everhorn.

"I'm just saying you look great, honey. That's all. It's still you . . . only different. Not a lot different, just a WOW kind of different."

Explosions were going off all around me. Here I thought I was being supportive, but every word was coming out wrong. I finally just had to raise the white flag and surrender. I told her I liked her blonde hair better, which I do, and that I couldn't wait until it was all colored back to normal.

But ladies, I have to pause for a moment and ask you—how are we guys supposed to respond to a situation like this? You make a change and if we like it, then that means we didn't like the way you used to be? And if we don't like it, then your self-esteem will somehow be shattered? With one trip to the beauty shop, you lead us into these minefields and then expect us to somehow navigate our way through them without any missteps. It's impossible.

If we like a change you've made to yourself, if we think it makes you look great, that's all we're saying when we brag on it. Don't read anything else between the lines. We can think you look good in your new look, or we can be perfectly happy with the way you are now. Make a change or stay the same, you look great to us either way. We love you with red hair, blonde hair, brunette hair, and no hair. We think you're a knockout in a dress, jeans, shorts, a bathing suit, lingerie, a hospital gown, or a muumuu. (Okay, maybe not a muumuu.) We married you, and no matter how many different looks you take on throughout the marriage, we're still going to love you. And when we think you look great, we want to tell you. So, please, cut us some slack.

Will Sherri ever do that to her hair again? Maybe, but we've made a pact between us. The next time she wants to get her hair colored, I'm getting mine colored, too. That way, we'll be a whole new couple. It's not that I want to color my hair, or that I want her to color hers again, but, you know . . . *whatever*.

THE RICK & BUBBA CODE
TO MARRIAGE ACCOUNTING

There is a system of accounting that has been passed down from generation to generation. Every married man knows about the existence of this account. But the actual account numbers, the pass code to get into the account, and the register to see each transaction, are a more closely guarded secret than the national nuclear codes.

We like to call this secret accounting system the "Rick and Bubba Code to Marriage Accounting." The Rick and Bubba Code to Marriage Accounting works like a bank account. Husbands must keep their own accurate records of all deposits and withdrawals made to the account, in case there is ever an error. The wife can keep her records, too, but it is the husband's responsibility to keep duplicate records because he stands to lose the most should an accounting dispute ever arise. Some women will conveniently forget to input some of the husband's deposits while at the same time conveniently doubling or even tripling their own deposits. Again, we're only saying *some* women. But since the majority of us husbands simply keep these figures in our heads (the same way the majority of us keep our checking account record in our heads), we can at times get seriously overdrawn in both our checking accounts and our marriage accounts. The only way for a husband to safeguard against this is to keep his own register.

This is how deposits and withdrawals are made into a typical Rick and

Bubba Marriage Account. Say you want to go hunting with your buddies. This would be considered a withdrawal from your marriage account. A fishing trip would be treated the same. However, seeing a chick flick or sitting through a play with your wife would be considered a credit, like making a deposit back into your bank account. In other words, doing something you enjoy but your wife doesn't is a withdrawal. Doing something your wife enjoys but you hate is a deposit. See how that works?

Some creative bookkeeping comes into play in situations such as "I'm going to take the kids hunting with me, but I'm not going to shoot anything." While technically this would be a withdrawal (you're on a hunting trip), you are taking the kids along with you, and that makes it a deposit, too. The entire excursion, in this case, would be a wash. It's neither a deposit nor a withdrawal. It's like cashing a check at the bank. Nothing actually goes into your account and nothing comes out of it. It's a simple transaction that doesn't affect your balance at all.

Occasionally, we both will be asked to appear on hunting shows on television. We maintain that these appearances should not count against us. Again hunting would normally be a withdrawal, but since we're working and all the hunting is done on camera, we say the experience should not count as a debit, but rather a credit. So far, our wives have agreed. Of course, they also think that making us go shopping with them to buy a dress for an event involving our work, or weddings, reunions, and other such gatherings on our side of the family, shouldn't be counted as a deposit either. True, we're still shopping, but they'll argue, in their twisted sort of way, that since it's on our side of the family, it's for our benefit. For the sake of peace, we'll give them that.

The following are some more examples of acceptable deposits and withdrawals for training purposes only:

DEPOSITS	WITHDRAWALS
Buying her jewelry	Selling off her jewelry
Doing the dishes	Using the dishes for skeet shooting
Dropping the kids off at school	Dropping the kids off at the wrong school

THE RICK & BUBBA CODE TO MARRIAGE ACCOUNTING

Telling her she's lost weight	Telling her to lose weight
Giving her a massage	Giving her a migraine
Sending her flowers	Mowing over her flowers
Taking the trash out to the curb	Taking your buddies out to a game
Reading marriage books together	Using marriage books to balance the uneven tool cart in the garage
Sending her mother to Hawaii	Making it a one-way ticket
Giving her a day at a spa for your anniversary	What anniversary?

We should also mention that a wife's method of recordkeeping in a marriage account is usually a marvel to behold. Not only will every single withdrawal of yours be noted and crosschecked, but she will have also written down what you were wearing when you made the withdrawal and what the weather was that day. Her recollection of your deposits, on the other hand, will be a bit more fuzzy. That is why your own accounting is vitally important. Without verifiable records, how can any wife see the true picture of her marriage? She may be showing your account as overdrawn when in reality you're half a deposit (you picked up one dirty sock off the floor) to the good.

THE RICK & BUBBA CODE TO JOINT HUNTING TRIPS

We don't want to compete with certain Middle Eastern countries in lighting or fanning the first embers of World War III, but we feel we need to address the delicate topic of bringing along wives on male hunting trips. Men who do this (we refer to them as "Wife-Bringers") think that they are making deposits into their marriage account, and that's one reason why they do it. This may be true, but they are also breaking an integral part of another long-standing code, which is the *No Wife-Bringer Code*. The No-Wife-Bringer Code only applies to guy hunting trips. You are free to bring your wife along on any other trip.

Don't misunderstand us here. We are absolutely fine with women hunters. That's not the issue. We believe that women have just as much of a right to hunt as men do. We just don't want them doing it at the same time we're trying to have some quality "guy" time. We don't hone in on your girls' night out. We don't beg you to take us to the nail salon with you, or to your luncheon date with your mother. We understand this is your time, and we happily leave you alone. Is it asking too much for you to let us guys have a little "me time" too?

There are certain things that we do when we're out hunting and fishing with a bunch of guys that we can't, or wouldn't, do when there are women around. We're talking about things that women would consider rude or crude. For example, if we happen to be suffering some gastrointestinal discomfort, we feel no qualms in relieving it. Nor do we feel pressure to put on different clothes every morning. Truth be told, we enjoy the freedom of wearing camo three days in a row and not shaving. We don't want the wife of one of our hunting buddies turning her nose up at our body odor, even if it is curling the hair on the buffalo head on the wall of the hunting lodge.

We can't find the exact verse in the Bible that covers this, but we are almost certain that bringing a wife along on a guys' hunting trip is a sin. We know it's not one of the regular Thou Shalt Nots, but we seem to recall the matter being hinted at somewhere near the beginning of the Bible, perhaps around the place where Eve tempted Adam to bite into that apple. It doesn't really say specifically that women aren't allowed on guy hunting trips, just like it doesn't really say it was an apple; but the commentary we read all but implied that the first couple may have been out on a hunting trip when all of this apple-bingeing happened. They weren't hunting for deer or anything like that because man didn't have to hunt for food back then. Perhaps Adam was out sizing up some of the game for later. Who knows? What we do know is his wife, Eve, distracted his attention and convinced him to take a bite of the forbidden fruit instead. He, of course, gave in to the temptation, and it's been downhill for mankind ever since. So you see, if only Eve hadn't gone hunting with Adam in the first place, everything would've stayed perfect.

But apparently, Adam was a "Wife-Bringer."

Deer Hunters Anonymous

Okay, maybe we're wrong about all that. But we are serious about our hunting. We can barely carry on a decent conversation with our wives without our minds drifting off to a whitetail weekend.

My (Rick) wife Sherri will be saying, "You know, honey, we've really got to go over our budget tonight," and I'll be thinking to myself, "Hey, is that a deer out there on the patio?" Or I'll get a phone call, "Mr. Burgess, we noticed that you haven't paid your electric bill in a few months and we were just wondering if there's a problem." About that time Lynyrd

Skynyrd's song "On the Hunt" will start playing in my head drowning out whatever the caller is saying, and I'll start looking for deer tracks all over the house. Of course, I'm sitting there in the dark by then, thanks to the electric company's shutting off our power, but even that doesn't stop me from my mission.

Bubba's even sicker than that. He can't look at a Santa's sleigh display at Christmas and not think to himself, *Hmmm . . . Dasher would go about 250.* When he takes down his Christmas tree, he'll part the branches to see if there's a deer on the other side.

I've got it so bad myself that I start picturing the mailman with antlers. When he drives up and sticks his head out of the mail truck, I'll go, "Yeah, he'll go about 225."

We don't want to get into the hunter vs. non-hunter discussion. We're just talking addiction here, pure and simple. If there is a 12-step program for us, we'll gladly sign up. We need some safe place where we can stand up and say, "Our names are Rick and Bubba and . . . is that a deer over there behind the file cabinet?"

We're finding deer scrapes everywhere we look. I think one reason we love hunting is because there's so much testosterone involved. It takes you back to the day when men had to hunt for their families. Back to the glory days when dads didn't change a single diaper or even go near a delivery room. No, we menfolk stayed out in the waiting room where there were television reruns and all the bad coffee you could drink. The chairs weren't comfortable, but us guys stretched out across them the best we could, knowing we were doing our part while our wives were in the other room birthing our offspring. It was the least we could do.

But then someone had to come along and decide that it really was the least we could do and then changed everything. Now, not only are we in the delivery rooms, we go to the doctor's appointments with our wives. And Lamaze classes. We go to parent/teacher meetings at our kids' schools; shoot, we even drive the carpool. And we're okay with all that. It took a little time to adjust, but we actually enjoy a lot of that stuff now.

But hunting is one thing that we can do where we still feel like real men. We're out there in camo, boots, our hair isn't combed, and we haven't shaved for days. We get to come back to the lodge at the end of the day and tell stories of the hunt. It's just us guys and we can tell our story the way we want to, without someone interrupting and correcting us that it wasn't really an 8-point buck that we saw peering around that tree, it was a raccoon. We don't have to deal with all those USCs (unnecessary story corrections). On an all-guy hunting trip we can tell our tales with whatever details we care to give and not be corrected every third word. We can once again feel like men.

So you see, it's nothing personal at all. We'd like to share more tips about this topic, but we think we just saw a scrape out on the patio. We've checked our marriage account balances and it looks like we've both got some hunting time coming. Of course, it'll use up all our points, so tomorrow we'll be watching *Out of Africa*.

Welcome to married life.

THE POWER OF A WOMAN

You've heard that men are from Mars and women are from Venus? Well, we want to bring the whole thing closer to home and explain our differences in a way you don't have to be an astronomer to understand. The way we see it, the difference between men and women's romantic energy is a lot like the difference between Christmas tree lights. There is the kind that won't work if one single light is out, and there is the kind that will still work no matter how many lights are out. For a woman, if one single bulb in the relationship is shorting out, the whole operation shuts down. For a guy, all sorts of bulbs can be burned out and he'll still light up with whatever's left.

Even so, women still hold most of the cards when it comes to romance. When we take our wives out for a romantic evening, the primary thing on our mind is how the evening is going to end. We honestly don't know. We dress up, put on cologne, and try our best to keep our fork out of our wife's plate for the entire meal (which isn't easy). We'll even go and get the car so our beloved won't have to walk the ten feet across the parking lot. All the while we're hoping and praying that the night will not be over.

Our wives, on the other hand, knew exactly how the evening is going to end. They know it when they're dressing, they know it when they're ordering their meal at the restaurant, they know it when they're having that last bite of dessert. How the evening ends will be no surprise to them.

That's a lot of power.

We husbands, on the other hand, are back to being in that elementary school classroom, sitting there with our Valentine bags, wondering if the girl of our dreams is going to drop us a little show of affection.

We're not sure how to change any of this, or if it even needs changing. We're just stating yet one more advantage to being a woman, and another disadvantage to being a man. Frankly, I think our wives keep us in the dark about how the evening is going to end on purpose. It's so we'll be on our best behavior at the restaurant. Or at least keep our fork to ourselves and our feet off the table.

PART III

DECODING PHYSICAL FITNESS

In our lifetime, we have witnessed several phenomena. We have watched eight-tracks morph into cassette tapes and LPs into CDs and MP3s. We have witnessed the invention of the microwave, VCRs, DVDs and HDTV. We've experienced the birth of ATM machines, and of bilingual ATM machines. We had game before the three-point-line. Shoot, we have even seen Madonna go from Bad Material Girl to kabbalah-preachin' children's book author.

But of all the trends we've seen come and go, one that has both pained and amused us is the physical fitness craze. Used to be, all a guy had to do to prove his manliness was go to work, tote the firewood, and open the pickle jar when called upon. These days, he's got to count carbs, do something called yoga, and not even think of eating any of those soon-to-be-outlawed-in-a-restaurant-near-you trans fats. And they've made the pickle jar a lot harder to get into.

Here are a few of our observations about all the sweating, pumping, and counting going on around us these days . . .

QUESTIONS WE'D LIKE TO ASK SKINNY PEOPLE

One of our favorite things to do is to talk to skinny people. Not only are they interesting, but you don't have to watch your food around a skinny person.

Since this book is poised to be a bestseller (all of Bubba's family promised to buy one), we thought we would take advantage of the exposure and ask the following questions to all you skinny people who might be reading this. These are questions that we've wondered about for years, and now we may finally get our answers.

1. Is eating not fun for you?

Excuse us for saying this, but whenever we see one of you skinny people eating, it doesn't look like you're having any fun. If you are having fun and you really do enjoy eating those bamboo shoots and alfalfa sprouts, you might want to start telling your face that because we've been watching you sitting there in your booth (the one you effortlessly slid into without having to rearrange the table) and we've got to be honest with you—you hardly ever smile. So come on, tell us. Are you happy? Are you really, really happy?

We only ask because we're happy. When we eat, it's a party. For years, thin people have been under the assumption that those of us who are overweight eat because we are hungry. Or we're depressed. Or we have some sort of chemical imbalance, can't deal with stress, or need an outlet for some deep psychological issue. That's not the case at all. We eat because the food just tastes good in our mouths. We eat because it's fun! We love our food. It makes us happy. Why do you think so many of us are so jolly? Hunger has very little to do with why we eat.

To further prove our point, I (Bubba) recently conducted an experiment: I ate an apple, then I followed it with a vanilla shake. Which one do you think tasted better? The vanilla shake, of course. Imagine that.

Now, we get how some people may live a lifetime of "choosing the apple"—or the carrot, or the wheat germ-tofu-portabello sandwich—*if* it's for ambition, career, or because your doctor, personal trainer, or mother is eating at the same restaurant you are. That's a sacrifice that world class athletes and Hollywood superstars must make to stay on top of their game. But, what we don't see, and what we won't believe is that a person in his or her right mind is going to pick healthy food over nonhealthy food and truly be happy about it. Someone might pick it, but it will be with a sense of regret.

Still don't believe us? Let's do the experiment right now. Given the choice, which of the following would *you* pick?

Rice Cakes	Little Debbie cakes
Tofu	Twinkies
Alfalfa sprouts	Almond Joy
Salmon	Snickers
Wheat germ topping	Whipped cream topping
Brussels sprouts	Butterfinger
Grains	Gravy
Seaweed	See's candy
Brie	Brownies
Leeks	Licorice

We rest our case. There's nothing to debate here. The column on the right is going to win hands down every time. Calories just taste better. While you skinny people are eating for sustenance, we're eating for the pure joy of it. So we ask you, who's having the better time? Where's the excitement in what you're doing? When's the last time you heard a dinner guest squeal with delight because you brought out cauliflower?

We don't order a milkshake because we need one. We order it because we know the celebration that's going to take place when that first lump of chocolate ice cream works its way up the straw.

That pie we consumed in one sitting last night had nothing to do with nutrition. We know that. But that pie was fun! Can the same thing be said about the bran you had for breakfast? Country-fried steak with mashed potatoes and a pool of gravy? Fun! Hot fudge sundae? Fun! Cinnamon rolls? Fun!

Hummus?

Exactly.

Not only do you skinny people not have fun eating, you haven't made eating a priority. It just isn't all that important to you. You can eat now or you can eat later. You can eat here or you can eat there. You can pass on dessert or you can take just a bite of it.

Now, up to this point, we've been patient with you. But it's time to talk turkey. And by this we mean deep fried. Those of you who can try the blood pressure machine at Walgreens and not have the alarms go off, who use an exercise show on television for more than dinner music, and who can order the entire Nutri System program for more than an appetizer to your regular meals, what's wrong with you? Do you have any idea how messed up your priorities are? And if so, are you finally in a place where you want to make a change? Have your eyes finally been opened to see that you're not getting enough fun in your diet? Far be it from us to judge, but you really do seem sad. We're concerned for you. Do you want to talk about it? Do you want to open up and share your pain with us? Are you going to finish those french fries . . . ?

2. Does it get as hot for you as it does for us?

If you are overweight, a hot day can get on you like a blanket. With every move you make, you feel like a beast of burden. Like an ox pulling a yoke. Believe us, children and small dogs could drown in the sweat that falls off our bodies on a typical August afternoon in Alabama.

What we would like to know is, does it feel the same to you? Do you skinny people feel heat the same way we do? Or do you go, "106 degrees? Love it! Bring it on!" Do you look forward to hot summer months so you can wear your skinny swim suits and get your skinny tans?

Tell us you feel the heat, too. That it's not just us. You owe us that much. After all, we both have been providing shade for a lot of you for years.

If we seem like we're coming across a little hard on skinny people, please forgive us. It's just that this is our book and, as you can tell, we've got a lot of frustration pent up inside of us. Skinny people have been having their say in books for years. Exercise books, diet books, health books, fashion. Now it's our turn.

3. Do you feel like you're wasting the time of those who put out buffets?

Are you uncomfortable with the term "all you can eat"? Think about it. Those cooks work hard. They wake up early in the morning and start preparing the food. They go to extreme lengths to make sure the serving trays stay full. And what do you do? You walk right on by, often not tasting a single bite of 90 percent of the dishes. How rude can you be? We take a scoop of everything just to show our appreciation. After all, if food is a party, then an all-you-can-eat buffet is the Inaugural Ball. Do you enjoy being a party pooper?

4. Why are you running down the street for no good reason?

We see you jogging down our streets in your skinny jogging suits. Why are you doing this? It seems so pointless. Where are you going? Usually you just turn around and head back home. Does this make sense to you? If you ever see us running, you'd better join us because it would only mean one thing—something horrible is chasing us.

But you? You seem to run for no reason at all. We could understand if you were running to the corner market to pick up milk and a loaf of bread. But we never see you running with milk and bread under your arm. Sometimes you'll be carrying some sort of weight thingy, but never groceries.

If you feel so compelled to sweat, we say make it for a good reason. "I baled hay today," or "I cleaned out the garage today," or "Honey, I'm wearing cologne tonight." Those are all good reasons to work up a sweat. Let your exercise mean something.

And what's with all that indoor exercise equipment? Why walk for twenty minutes on a treadmill just to end up in the exact same place that you started?

It seems like such a waste.

On that same note, why are you riding bicycles that go nowhere? A stationary bike is just that—stationary. Did you not catch that in the name? Why are you climbing up on this contraption that has only one wheel and pretending it's something it's not? It's not really a bicycle. The meter might indicate that you just rode five miles, but they're *pretend* miles. You're still in your living room.

It's like counting in dog years. You can say your dog's lived seven years for every year of his life, but in reality, he's really just lived one year for every year. If he is 17, that doesn't mean he's 119. It means he is 17. Dogs just don't live as long as humans do. We never counted Howdy Doody's age in puppet years, did we?

Now for those of you who are real bicyclists, and ride real miles, we just have one thing to say: What's with the outfit? Couldn't they have at least picked out a cooler looking helmet for you to wear? No offense, but that one looks like you're wearing a turtle on your head. No wonder there was such a heated debate over whether bicyclists should have to wear helmets. The bicyclists were fighting for their dignity.

5. Is that power bar really good?

Be honest. Can it compare to a Milky Way? Of course not. The reason they call it a power bar is because it tastes like you're chewing through electrical wiring.

6. What's it like to tuck your shirt in?

That looks like fun. We like how the shirt goes into the pants like that. It's a neat and snappy look. What's that feel like? We don't know. We've never been able to do that.

7. What's it like to get on an airplane and not have everyone fear you're going to sit down next to them?

Is it nice to board a plane and not see everyone drop their head at the same time and pretend to be asleep? We may make the seat a little tight for you skinny people, but we don't enjoy hearing you smacking on your apples and Trail Mix for the entire flight either.

8. What's it like to wear corduroy pants without fearing you'll be starting a fire?

Enough said.

9. Do you ever sweat?

We have watched you working out, but we've noticed you never seem to sweat. Is that normal? Have you ever had that checked out?

Sweating is something the body does naturally to cool itself down. We cool ourselves down with a carton of Ben and Jerry's. If you find you can't sweat no matter what you try, try a carton of Ben and Jerry's (not ours, get your own). It is important for you to maintain a normal body temperature. Rocky Road helps us do this.

10. What's it like to get to pick clothes and not feel like you're settling?

I (Rick) was a fat kid. My brother Greg was a skinny kid. I used to resent the fact that whenever we'd go school clothes shopping, Greg would have all these unbelievable choices to pick from—Jordache, Wrangler, Levi's. All he had to do was find the jeans he liked, and they'd have four or five pairs in his size—and different colors, too.

Me? I'd have to go over to the "Husky" section, where the selection was a lot more limited. I could choose between a pair of jeans with a stripe on the pocket or a pair without. And that's if they even had the jeans in my size.

While we're on the subject of clothes, I think Bubba and I need to speak to a few fashion issues in our own camp.

Some of us on the larger side are continuing to wear certain trendy clothes no matter how ridiculous they may look on us. Allow us to make a suggestion here. Just because a bare midriff is in style, that doesn't mean we all have to join in. The Bible even covers this one: "All things are lawful; but not all things are expedient" (1 Corinthians 10:23 ASV). I believe this would include stirrup pants, too. This is a hard and fast Rick and Bubba Rule: Stirrup pants can make some people look like they're riding a horse that we can't see.

We've found that the best look for us is a T-shirt that's one size bigger than what we normally wear. We'll wear that for about a month or so, then buy one that's two sizes bigger. Then three sizes bigger. This way, we can continue to eat whatever we want while people keep asking us if we've lost weight.

We have other questions we'd like to ask skinny people, but we'll leave it here for now. What we love most is when a skinny single guy will be eating a carrot and working out as hard as he can, and then he'll see the two of us walk by in the shape that we're in, with our two beautiful wives on our arms. At that moment you know he's got to be asking himself, *is it worth it?* We're telling you, all you single fellas out there, get off that treadmill. You could fall and hurt yourself. Toss that tofu in the trash and start cracking a few jokes instead. A good sense of humor is what women love. It's one of the secrets of the Rick and Bubba Code. We could have shared that gem with you a long time ago and saved you a fortune on health club fees.

But you wouldn't sit next to us on that airplane, remember?

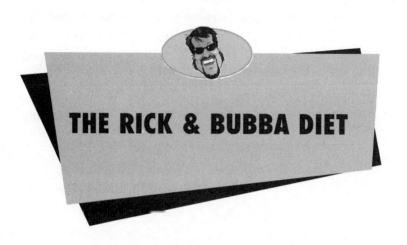

THE RICK & BUBBA DIET

It goes without saying that you don't get to be the "two sexiest fat men alive" by being slim. Slim is not our goal. We are satisfied with, and even proud of our "two sexiest fat men alive" title. We've worked hard to get that. Especially the "alive" part. Neither one of us likes to go on diets. We don't mind losing weight, but we would rather do it our own way.

Our way is to not know we're on a diet. If someone says, "We're going to put you on a diet," it'll never work. We'd rebel. The only way we can lose weight is to trick ourselves into thinking that everything is normal, when in reality we're cutting back "just a little" or "exercising just a little bit more." We just don't know it. It doesn't take much of an adjustment in our lifestyle for us to lose weight. We can lose three pounds by just walking a little farther to the buffet. Another two will drop off of us if we skip the ice cream with our usual chocolate cake—or at least the sprinkles on the ice cream with our cake.

Little changes like that bring big rewards. In fact, since the writing of our last book Bubba has lost thirty-three pounds, and I have lost thirty pounds. But neither one of us were aware that we were "on a diet." We weren't doing Tae Bo; we were just scaling back. Eating three slices of cornbread instead of six. Baby steps.

Everyone knows that the secret to weight loss is to burn off more calories than you take in. That's a no-brainer. It's the same as with finances. To get ahead financially, you've just got to spend less than you earn. It's that simple. So for us to lose weight, we merely have to change a few habits, all without letting ourselves know about it. This can be tricky. It has also cost us some good commercial accounts. I can't tell you how many diet companies have asked us to go on their diet and be their spokespersons. But it'd never work because we're pretty sure there's a "no cheating" clause in the contract.

The exercise clause in most of these contracts would trip us up a bit, too. We'll exercise, but like with the diet, we don't want to know we're exercising. If you put us on a treadmill and turn it on, we'll just step off of it. But put us on a basketball court for a game of 21, and we're in for the long haul. Don't sign us up for a 10 K race. Set a pit bull after us, and we'll break every running record known to man. Don't buy us a set of weights. Buy us a big screen television set and tell us to help the delivery men bring it into the house. Or ask us to move our recliner from the den into the living room, or better yet, into the dining area, and exchange it for our regular chair. We're all for that kind of weightlifting.

Some of us are just a little more philosophical. We want our exercise to have meaning. We don't mind sweating; there just has to be a purpose to it. Like malaria.

So to summarize, here are the only three reasons why we will ever exercise:

1) Sports
2) If our lives are in grave danger, or
3) If we're asked to lift heavy objects that will in some way bring luxury to our lives.

Oh, and maybe there's a fourth reason. Marital romance. That's an acceptable way to exercise too. But 9 out of 10 doctors recommend turning off the treadmill first.

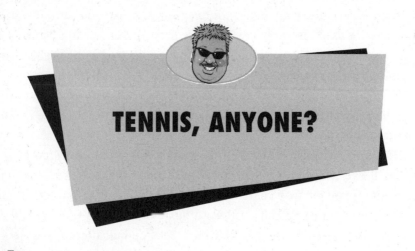

TENNIS, ANYONE?

A few years ago while Betty and I were on vacation, we decided to have a little fun and play a round of tennis on the hotel tennis courts. Personally, I could have thought of other fun things to do at a hotel with my wife (their brunch was supposed to be great), but Betty wanted to play tennis.

So we drove to a local Wal-Mart and bought a couple of inexpensive tennis rackets. (I don't know if you realize this or not, but shopping for exercise equipment also counts as exercise. It's true. Driving to a gym to sign up for a membership also counts. In fact, these will be the only calories you'll burn out of your gym membership because everyone knows that once you sign up at a gym, you never go.)

Now I don't mean to brag, or to embarrass my lovely wife in any way, but when we got out on the tennis courts, Betty made me look like Andre Agassi. She hardly hit the ball at all. It was an easy win, too easy, but I held back from rubbing it in. I would never do anything like that.

So after Betty was toast, she determined that she was going to sign up for tennis lessons as soon as we got home. She even joined a team. She even became captain of the team. And within a year, she led her team to win the state championship!

In that same amount of time, I went from being a decent tennis player to having two knee surgeries and months of physical therapy trying to keep up with her. But I was happy for Betty. She worked hard for that state championship. And honestly, it didn't sting my pride all that much. After all, how good can she really be? To this day, whenever we play tennis she still can't seem to hit the ball anywhere near where I'm standing.

THE RICK & BUBBA
EXERCISE VIDEO

Due to reasons beyond our control, the release of the *Rick and Bubba Exercise Video* has been delayed. The problem arose during the layout process of the "Before" and "After" pictures. It was then that someone noticed that the "Before" picture actually showed us looking slimmer than the "After" picture. For some reason this was not what producers of the exercise video were looking for, and so the release of the *Rick and Bubba Exercise Video* has been indefinitely postponed.

We realize many of you had been putting off starting your own exercise program until our new video was available, and we do apologize for this inconvenience. You will have to stay in your recliner a little longer until this problem can be remedied.

This isn't the only trouble we've had with the release of our new exercise video. One environmental group tried to say that the sight of the two of us in Spandex will require a label on the video warning that anyone with even the slightest level of vision may be in danger of dizziness, headaches, or stroke. This issue is working its way through the rating system even as we write.

Another problem we've run (figuratively, of course) into is the fact that most other exercise videos involve some level of movement. As many of you know, this is not our style. We felt it was high time to buck this ridiculous trend in exercise videos. What's more, we like to give our fans what they've come to expect of us, and so we insisted on the *Rick and Bubba Exercise Video* being the first stationary workout program on the market. We are pleased to say that not a single calorie was burned or harmed in the making of the video. But producers of the video disagreed with this, too, and insisted we do it their way.

This, in our opinion, is a deal breaker. When we agreed to make the exercise video, no one mentioned that real "exercise" would be involved. We have an image to uphold. We are the two sexiest fat men alive, and we won't let an exercise video jeopardize that title.

So until this matter is settled, we will not be releasing our exercise video to the public. We know many of you are disappointed, but we're not about to move from our position because, well, that too would be movement and that's exactly our point.

PART IV

DECODING POLITICS

It's no secret that politically we both lean a little to the conservative side of things. It's not so much a conviction as it is a matter of which political party puts on the best dinners. The Democrats have a lot more health fanatics, so we tend to leave their gatherings still hungry. The Republicans, on the other hand, know how to eat. "Our party won! Let's put on a dinner." "Our party lost! Let's put on a dinner." "Tax bill passed! Let's put on a dinner." "Tax bill failed! Let's put on a dinner." They put on a dinner for everything! We can't think of a better reason to align ourselves with the Republican party.

Now, we realize a few Democrats are independent eaters. Bill Clinton and Ted Kennedy seem to march to the beat of a different fork. But generally speaking, Republicans win the banquet vote hands down.

Independents try to have it both ways. They'll have dinners that aren't quite as health conscious as the Democratic dinners, but they're a little too noncommittal. They'll serve salmon with macaroni and cheese. Can you trust a party like that?

That's why we prefer Republican political rallies. Some of it has to do with our convictions, yes.

But mainly, it's the chow.

FIX WHAT'S BROKEN AND LEAVE THE REST ALONE

No matter which party happens to be in office, we think we have some suggestions and thoughts on how things could improve in this country:

For starters, we are for term limits. For everyone. Not just politicians, but in the work force, too. Even food has freshness dates. There's nothing worse than people being in their job long after their enthusiasm has expired. Teachers, bus drivers, television news reporters, waiters—all of them should be forced to retire once they start hating to show up for their jobs.

And any politician who would rather be anywhere else but sitting in his or her congressional seat voting on important issues that are going to affect the future of our nation, then it's time for them to move on, too. Political positions were never meant to be lifelong careers anyway. Serve the people for a few years, then go back to your regular job, knowing that you've made a difference in your country. People who have grown so weary of their job that it's affecting how they do it should do us all a favor and find another line of work.

Another thing we feel would improve our country is a flat 10 percent income tax across the board. If 10 percent is good enough for God, it should be good enough for the government. Since the government and creditors think we can live on 10 percent of our money, let's let them try living on 10 percent of it for a while. Our founding fathers would be shocked at how much we're taxed today and even more shocked that we're taking it. (They'd also be shocked at *Desperate Housewives*, but that's a whole different issue.)

And forget all this talk about "tax cuts for the rich." Tax cuts should be for everybody. But keep in mind that politicians are rich people. When they campaign on being "for the common man," they are not the common man. But that's okay. There's nothing wrong with someone having wealth. A rich person gave me my job. A rich person probably gave you your job, too. They give a lot of people their jobs. And when rich people are squeezed, they are going to squeeze back, right on down the line.

As for our foreign policy, we believe in peace through strength. If you've got the means to win a war, then win it. Otherwise, don't go to war.

We would also like to see The Separation of Church and State controversy cleared up once and for all. Did you know that the Separation of Church and State was first implemented by Thomas Jefferson in order to assure a Baptist church that the government wouldn't interfere with them? It wasn't to protect the State from the influence of the Church. It was to protect the Church from the interference of State. Somehow we've gotten it all turned around.

Finally, we suggest that someone make backpedaling illegal in Congress. If a congressman votes for something, he shouldn't be allowed to change his stance when talking to the press. If a congresswoman really has made a policy shift, then she needs to say, "I was wrong (gasp!) when I voted and have now changed my mind." At the very least, any member of Congress who makes a huge stand FOR something only to come out later AGAINST it, should be forced to wear flip-flops and ride a unicycle while on the floor. That way, at least the backpeddling would serve a purpose.

We have plenty more suggestions, and should any of the political parties wish to hear them, we're happy to address them . . . provided there's a dinner.

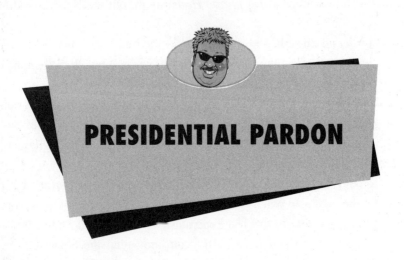

PRESIDENTIAL PARDON

In *The Da Vinci Code*, a painting of the *Mona Lisa* is a key part of the mystery. In the Rick and Bubba Code, the key is a photograph. Three of them, really. One is of us at a fish fry. The others are of President George W. Bush with Rick and his wife, Sherri, and of the president with me and my wife, Betty.

The last two are the topic of this chapter.

How did we luck into that honor? Maybe it's because of our conservative political leaning. Maybe it's because we have our own radio audience packed with potential voters. Maybe it's simply because the president had some extra film. Whatever the reason, when the president came to Birmingham to speak at a fund-raising dinner, Rick and I were given the opportunity to pose with the Big Guy.

Many people at this event had paid good money to get their picture taken with the commander in chief. But without the connections or the big donation, Rick and I had to arrange our presidential photo opportunity the old-fashioned way: We had to beg.

It worked. Arrangements were made for our picture to be taken with the president after the fund-raising dinner. We tried our best to play down the invitation to the rest of the people in our party—we didn't want to make them feel bad.

"Gosh, it's such a hassle to go up there and stand in that long line," we said. "We'd really rather sit here and have some more of these finger foods with all of you. But we can't keep the president waiting."

While standing in the photo line, we had time to do the math. Most of the other people standing in that line had paid $50,000 for their photo, which added up to a lot of money. A LOT of money. We weren't surprised when the news reported that the Alabama event was the largest political fund-raising event held by a sitting president to date. Knowing that gave us a sense of pride. Sometimes the rest of the country tends to look down their noses a bit at the South. Like we all had to hock our double-wides to attend such an event. But there's plenty of money down here, proven by the fact that this little fund-raiser put some $3.8 million dollars in their kitty that day. And the event was put together in only three weeks—or twice as long as some Hollywood marriages!

Now, just so you know, getting your picture taken with the president is a little like being in a two-second movie. They have a mini set there, complete with a little carpet, flags, and a nice background. You can't see the president at first because there are blinders partitioning off the area. But every once in a while a couple of flashes go off, and the line moves up a little more.

When we finally did get close enough to catch a glimpse of him, I have to say it was a little surreal. Seeing the president of the United States standing there in plain view hits you more than you think it would. All you can do is go, "Wow, this is the president." It doesn't really matter who it is standing there, you're just in awe of the office itself. In my mind, I started thinking about all the others who have stood in that place—John Fitzgerald Kennedy, Ronald Reagan, Abraham Lincoln, all of the great people who have held that position of honor and responsibility. Some may not have lived up to the position, but you've still got to be in awe of the office. And when you're in line about to meet a president of the United States, it really does get to you. It's an all-encompassing, almost spiritual moment.

So there we were, continuing to work our way to the front of the line. As we looked at him, all Rick and I could think about was that this is the guy who on September 11 had to make all those decisions. Split-second decisions that would affect an entire nation, and ultimately the whole world. And the word reached him about the attack while he was talking to a room full of elementary school students. He had to make decisions that would affect the future, while the future was looking him right in the face.

Finally, it was our turn for our presidential photo. Rick told Betty and me to go first, so we walked up to the president and shook his hand. I had wanted to leave an impression on the president. I wanted to say something so brilliant that he would say, "Bill, I want you to come back with us to the White House for dinner. You can stay in the Lincoln bedroom. Bring the family. We'll have a fish fry." I wanted him to know who we were. That we were Rick and Bubba from Alabama. I wanted to say something funny and witty and profound.

But when the moment finally came, it no longer mattered who we were. It didn't even matter if we left an impression on him at all. All that came into my mind to say was, "I know you hear this all the time, but we're praying for you. And I appreciate the way you share your faith."

The president stopped and just looked at me for what seemed like ten minutes. In reality, it was probably just a few seconds. Then he said, "I appreciate that. Never stop praying for me. I need it."

It was one of those moments where you almost get teary-eyed. I could hear a marching band playing "Hail to the Chief" and see hundreds of balloons falling from the ceiling. None of that was really happening, but for me, that's what the moment was like. I'll never forget it.

It was also at this precise moment that the lovely Betty was getting into position on the other side of the president for our photo. Now I should mention that when Betty gets nervous, she goes into full laughter mode. And for this, Betty was extremely nervous. All of a sudden, she started giggling uncontrollably. She was standing with the president of the United States, and she was acting like she was on some kind of laughing gas. It tickled the president and he started laughing and asked, "What's wrong?" Betty just said, "This is wild!" Now they were both laughing. The photographer snapped the picture and, of course, Betty blinked. She was laughing too hard to keep her eyes open. We had to do another one. But by then the president was laughing so hard, it encouraged Betty to keep going. She knew she had his attention, so in her nervousness, she started doing a comedy routine of sorts. (I should mention that this was shortly after the news reported that the president had choked on a pretzel.)

Betty said, "Mr. President, don't worry. I'm in the front row today. If you get choked or have any trouble, I'm a nurse and I'll be here."

The president laughed and said, "Where were you when I needed you?" Then he added, "I wish my dog had known how to take care of me."

By this time I had already walked off the carpet. But Betty had the president's ear, and she wouldn't let go. He wasn't even looking at me anymore. The two of them continued their little comedy act, while Rick and I helplessly looked on.

Rick told me later that while he was standing there, all he heard the president say was something like, "I wish my dog would treat me a little better." He was wondering what in the world Betty had just said to the president of the United States. Once he heard the story, he realized that the president had no doubt just meant that he wished his dog had known the Heimlich.

Both of those pictures now hang in the offices of the Rick and Bubba studio. They're two of our favorite pictures. If you look closely at them, some say that a key clue to the secret Rick and Bubba Code is hidden there. In some strange kind of mirror-imaged text, it is written:

Where is the dessert table?

THE FIRST DEPARTMENT
OF TRANSPORTATION

History doesn't record his name, but one morning long ago some guy woke up late for wherever he needed to be, saw a horse grazing in the grass and thought to himself, *Why, I do believe that creature could hold me!* Then, in an effort to make up for lost time, and before he could talk himself out of it, he jumped on the back of one very surprised creature and proceeded to try to ride him. The horse must have tried bucking him off at first, but the man hung in there and eventually broke him.

Can't you just picture that scene? We can almost hear the man yelling back to all the onlookers as he rode past them, "Never walk again!"

You've got to admire someone like that. It takes a certain degree of intelligence and want of adventure to see a four-legged animal standing there minding his own business and then say to yourself, *The next time I catch that horse eating grass and he's not looking, I'm up there!*

It makes you wonder, too, about the animals that man tried to ride before the horse. . . . You can almost see a group of guys sitting around the campfire discussing it one night: "Well, my vote says we don't try the mountain lion again. He didn't much go for it the last time."

And you know the thought of riding cows had to have crossed somebody's mind. After all, they're slower, easier to catch up to if you fall off, and, hey, free milk.

THE FIRST DEPARTMENT OF TRANSPORTATION

For faster transportation, someone must have eyed the buffalo. They're fast, but as we're sure the rider soon discovered, they don't come with brakes. You know that's why the settlers kept moving west. The guy who first tried riding a buffalo couldn't get him to stop. When the exhausted creature finally keeled over, the settlers decided to stay and live right there. That's why we have people living in Nevada today. You think they would have stayed in 117-degree heat if the buffalo could have made it four or five hundred more miles to the beach?

Some wilderness man up in the mountains had to have tried riding a bear. Looked out his hovel on the ridge and said, "We're getting so much use out of the horse and the buffalo, let's find us a bear to ride! Just think of all the stuff it could carry!"

Relatively speaking, a bear would be like a Winnebago compared to a horse. Of course, every time the bear stood up, it'd be about a ten-foot drop, but to a woman of that day, that was probably a small price to pay for more luggage space.

After about the sixth guy got eaten, though, someone must have gone to the seventh and said, "You know, we just aren't making any progress here. Take the saddle off that Grizzly and let's try something else."

A donkey could have been offered next. You know there had to have been doubts, though. "Aw, that thing can't hold anybody."

"Well, I'm going to give it a shot because it's a lot easier than gettin' up on that stupid bear, and at least he won't eat me."

So, the adventurers tested the donkey and soon discovered that, like the horse, it worked . . . that is, until they packed it up for the first trip and discovered it wouldn't budge.

"What's with this?" they must have said. "We have teenagers who are this stubborn. Who needs a traveling donkey bucking us, too?"

In other parts of the world, people were no doubt doing the same thing with camels. They were looking at those humped creatures and saying, "Hey, now there's a beast that'll take us somewhere. And looky there, it's already got a built-in bucket seat. God wouldn't have included that in the design if He didn't want us sitting up there on it."

When somebody over in Africa looked at the elephant, he had to have said, "Look, man, the whole world's out there riding animals. But those beasts can't touch the elephant. If we can figure out a way to get up there on him, we win!"

Then another dude saw a giraffe and said, "No, that's the perfect ride. If we can break the giraffe, look where we can hang all of our jackets and stuff—right there off those two little handlebar thingys sticking out the side of its head. Never again will our clothes wrinkle before we get to where we're going!"

(Does anyone know what those handlebar thingys are anyway? And why don't we humans have any? A couple of handlebars sticking out the sides of our foreheads would really come in handy. We'd never lose our car keys again.)

The giraffe would have been the perfect animal to domesticate, too. Think about how much help they could be around the house. We could get old "Spots" to clean out the gutters. And he'd really come in handy putting up Christmas lights and getting the star on top of the Christmas tree.

History may have a different take on all of this. Since that's the class where we got most of our sleep, we can't say for sure if we're right or not, but one thing we know is this: Every one of us who has ever ridden a horse, driven a car, flown in an airplane, or used any other means of transportation owes a debt of gratitude to these brave men and women who wanted to get somewhere a little faster and had the courage to try something different. If it wasn't for them, we'd all still be walking. Healthier perhaps, but a lot more tired.

THE RICK & BUBBA CODE
TO FOREIGN AFFAIRS

There is a growing campaign to get us to run for political office. We realize that Washington could benefit from two fresh voices. But we kind of like only putting in a few hours of work a day.

Maybe we could run for vice president.

We do have a lot of thoughts on our nation's foreign policy, though. And since it could be a while before our Oscar speech, we thought we'd go ahead and share those with you now.

Let's Pay Our Own Tab Before Tipping Others

First of all, why do we send so much of our hard-earned money overseas when we have important needs right here at home? We should be keeping America's resources here in our own backyard! Then we'll all have enough money to put it into supporting American goods like Japanese electronics, oil from Argentina, and small appliances from Germany.

Second, we want to say that we support world peace and think that whoever is in charge should be doing everything in their power to achieve it. In other words, tell those Hollywood celebrities to quit with all the feuds. (Angelina, leave Jen alone. And vice-versa. And Donald and Rosie, enough already!)

Another thing we'd like to say is that the United Nations isn't the answer to the world's problems. It doesn't even have that great of a snack bar.

We believe that we should always learn from our enemies, too. For instance, who built Saddam's television stations? We've both worked in television for years. We've gone off the air with the slightest power surge. But with coalition forces bombing Saddam's hideouts for weeks, he was still broadcasting. Remember that? That's the most incredible engineering crew we've ever seen. Who made their transmitter?

Forget Iraq's oil. Let's find out their broadcasting secrets!

PART V

DECODING FAMILY

Family. You can't live with them.

You can't live without them.

You can't ever get in the bathroom.

Family life has changed a lot in this country. Not only do we have working moms, stay-at-home dads, surrogate children, blended families, and Dr. Phil, we also have evolved into a society where fathers are expected to be, well, involved.

Men are more than the breadwinners and protectors of their homes; now we gotta change diapers, coach Little League, and express our feelings.

So what's our response to all this enlightenment? Who knows! We're too tired and depressed to think about it.

BEFORE YOU KNOW IT, THEY'LL BE DRIVING

There are five children in the Burgess household. They all have nick-names. It was my idea. Our oldest child is Brandi. When Brandi started showing some athletic prowess, I felt she needed a marketable nickname. Never mind the fact that she was just a child. I was looking ahead. Bubba thought "Jo Jo Burgess" sounded good, so the nickname stuck.

Our son Blake became "Boomer." He wasn't as intense as his sister.

His nickname was earned at a Little League game. When he was on deck about to go up to bat I told him, "Son, there are two outs and two men on base. We need you to get a huge hit so we can score and win this game."

He looked at me with all the sincerity of Babe Ruth, then looked up to heaven prayerful-like and said, "Dad, is that the Big Dipper or the Little Dipper?"

He did end up getting a huge hit, so after that we started calling him "Boomer."

Brooks was a big, loveable and loving toddler. Almost too loving. He would go after other children and love them to the ground. His love was overwhelming. So we started calling him "Big Love." And still do.

Brody got the nickname of "Taz." That about says it all. You know the Looney Tunes character, the Tazmanian Devil, who is always spinning out of control destroying everything in his path with his enthusiasm and hyperactivity? That's Brody. He doesn't mean to. He just can't control his energy yet. He's constantly dressing up as superheroes or playing pirate and banging your shin with his plastic sword.

Finally, there's "Cornbread" (Bronner). He's the baby. When he was six months old he decided that he was done with baby food. I put some cornbread on his high chair tray and there was no turning back. He loved it (like any good Southerner).

He's redheaded and when he's dressed in his overalls and no shirt, he looks a little like Opie.

Because of their energy level, Brooks and Brody (Big Love and Taz) have a second nickname. We call them the Killer B's. At the time of the following story they were six and four years of age.

Now, I'll be the first to admit that our boys can be a handful. I'll also admit that Sherri and I are not perfect parents. We do our best, but like every one of you parents reading this book, we have made our share of parenting errors. We try to correct them as quickly as possible and vow to do better the next time, but five children will take the pigment right out of anybody's hair.

At this particular time, Big Love was on a swimming team. He had advanced beyond the jumping-in-and-immediately-jumping-out-screaming-"There're sharks in the water" stage, and was actually beginning to hold his own in the swim meets.

This one particular swim meet was at a new facility. It was a country club in a neighboring community. It wasn't one of those uppity country clubs; I would call it medium uppity. Just uppity enough to where my family's arriving was sure to be a bit of a culture shock for some of the club members. My family is best served by the public pool, or simply the river.

But we weren't at the river, so we tried our best to be as inconspicuous as possible. The staff was warm in welcoming us to the facilities. (They did this out of view of the other patrons, but I don't think it was intentional.)

While that was going on, I looked up and caught a glimpse of a golf cart that someone had left near the area where we were standing. I noticed that the boys, Taz and Big Love, had climbed up into the golf cart and were now sitting in it. I excused myself from the staff, walked over, and said as directly as I could, "Let's get out, boys, because it's dangerous to be in a golf cart without an adult."

"Daddy, can you give us a ride?" one of them begged.

"No, it's not my golf cart," I said. "I can't just get in that thing and ride you around."

"Pleeeeeeeeeeeeeease!" Taz said.

"Pleeeeeeeeeeeeeease!" Big Love echoed.

I remained firm.

"Everybody get out now!"

To my amazement, they did.

There's a feeling of pride that wells up inside you whenever your offspring follow your commands. You feel like a noble drill sergeant, only you don't make them snap to attention and salute. But we're working on that.

Anyway, pleased that my boys had removed themselves from the potential hazard, I felt free to converse with the people standing around me.

It was about this time that I became, let's see, how did I put it in the accident report? Oh yes, "distracted." Someone came up and started talking to me as I was gathering up our towels, so my mind was clearly off the golf cart.

Unfortunately, Taz and Big Love's minds weren't.

Now, I should set the stage for this story just a little bit. The golf cart, exhibit number one, was parked on an incline, facing up the hill. I had told the boys to remove themselves from the vehicle and stand at my side. They had done this.

But if that was the case, then what was that sound of children laughing I heard in the distance, apparently from the vicinity of the golf cart?

I knew even before I turned around what I was about to see. I felt it in my gut. It was one of those moments when you know disaster is looming and you're already trying to figure out a way to fix it.

I looked down and saw that the kids were nowhere near me. Then I looked at the golf cart, now rolling merrily down the road and picking up speed. At last I caught a glimpse of the boys. In the golf cart. The golf cart that I had told them to stay out of. They weren't acting scared in the least. Not of the danger they faced riding in an unmanned golf cart. Not of the danger they faced with me.

Let me tell you, it's a weird place you find yourself in when you look up and see your four- and six-year-olds driving down the street. I didn't want my children injured or killed. I also didn't want any pedestrians crossing the street getting injured or killed. But there was nothing to stop their acceleration. It was apparent that they were going to keep going for a while unless they somehow turned the cart and rammed into a parked car.

So there you are in this weird place, hoping for the lesser of two evils. You're actually praying that your children will ram their golf cart into someone's very nice SUV. It's the safest way to stop them, you figure.

Their swimming coach, Cal, saw the predicament the boys were in and actually joined me in running after the golf cart—as if we could catch up to it. But that's what Super Dads do. You do whatever it takes. In moments like this, instinct simply kicks in.

But I needed more than instinct that day. I needed God's help, and let me tell you, Taz and Big Love's guardian angel was looking out for them, as he does every day. Needless to say, their guardian angel is a very tired angel.

The funniest part of this whole story was watching their joyful, giggling faces transform after they hit a car and came to a stop. Their ear-to-ear smiles immediately changed to an "Uh-oh" face frozen in time. They hit an SUV wide open, and then they looked up and saw me. I had finally caught up to them and was just standing there shaking my head in disbelief. They knew what I was thinking. I knew they knew what I was thinking. I was thinking, *As soon as I know they are fine, I am going to kill them!* Not literally, but I was absolutely furious! They had disobeyed a direct order from their father.

Now I was so focused on disciplining them that I didn't even care about the car they had just hit. I would deal with the aftermath of what they had done later. Right now, I had to get them out of the golf cart, and they were going to get it. Taz would be first. He was the youngest, and it appeared he was also the designated driver. Then it was going to be Big Love's turn.

I wrote out a note for the car they hit and thanked the country club members and staff (who were looking on in horror) for their hospitality. And then we walked on to our car.

Driving home, I asked the kids, "Do you realize the severity of what you've done? Are you getting this?"

Taz presented his defense first, "I didn't do it, Dad."

I said, "Son, you were driving. You were behind the wheel. You were the one who turned the wheel and cut into that SUV. How can it not be at least partially your fault?"

"I wasn't the one who took off the brake."

"But you were a participant. And you were loving it! Does the word 'Whee!' sound familiar to you? You could have gotten yourselves killed!"

"We didn't get hurt."

"That's not the point! The point is you were both told not to get in that golf cart, but you got in it anyway. What were you thinking?"

"We just thought it would be awesome."

"What?!"

"You know, awesome."

"Well, was it awesome when you got disciplined?" I said.

"No," they said. "You're not going to tell Momma, are you?"

I told them I had to, because there was some property damage involved that we were going to have to pay for.

They seemed to be sufficiently ashamed of themselves, and the SUV really hadn't sustained that much damage. But I haven't been back to that country club since. It was pretty nice, and I really wouldn't mind joining it someday. But sometimes it's just best to give people time to forget your face.

FIRE IN MY LOINS
(IT'S NOT WHAT YOU THINK)

It didn't make the evening news, but only because there were no casualties. Well, there was one—a material witness to the event. Maybe I should start at the beginning.

The unfortunate incident took place one morning while I was trying to get ready for work. As always, I had gotten up early and stepped into the shower. Everything was going fine up to that point. Even the shower went well. But when I finished and went looking for a clean pair of underwear to put on, I discovered there weren't any. Not in the drawer. Not on the dresser. Not on the floor. Nowhere.

I thought briefly about recycling an old pair, but we were right in the middle of an Alabama summer and, well, recycling underwear in that kind of heat and humidity is frankly against the law.

Wondering if there were any clean underwear in the dryer, I walked to the laundry room and looked. There weren't, but I checked in the washer and did find a clean pair rolled up like a croissant between a couple of T-shirts and some socks. But they, along with the rest of the load, were still wet.

Knowing I needed to hurry up and leave for the station, I had to figure out a way to dry the underwear fast. The idea of using a blow dryer crossed my mind, but I didn't want to wake up the whole house.

That's when it hit me. The microwave! I could put the wet underwear in the microwave! If a microwave could cook a potato, popcorn, and an entire roast in mere minutes, it had to be able to dry a pair of underwear in no time flat.

I was a genius!

I popped the underwear in the microwave, set the timer, and turned it on. While the carousel turned, I ran upstairs to brush my teeth. There wasn't a minute to spare. Besides, it was perfectly fine to leave it.

I was an idiot!

I'm not sure if it was the smoke, the sparks, or the buzzer going off that first caught my attention. Whatever it was, I am to this day still in awe of what a microwave can do to a perfectly good pair of underwear. It burned a hole right through them! (I probably should have known when I didn't see a designated button marked "Underwear" between the ones marked "Popcorn" and "Beverage" that I was only asking for trouble. But I was in too much of a hurry to think rationally.)

So for those of you keeping score, the end result was:

Microwave – 1

Bubba – 0

I had flambéed my Fruit of the Loom! Now, I had no choice but to go ahead and wear them to work. It turned out okay, though. I don't think anyone noticed.

But an awful lot of people did keep asking me if I'd taken up smoking.

A GEORGIA SAFARI

One of my favorite vacation destinations is in Pine Mountain, Georgia—a place called Calloway Gardens. The grounds are beautiful, and we usually stay at a nice summer cottage there.

Near Calloway Gardens is another place that we've discovered. It's a wild animal park that you can actually drive through in your car and see the animals. My wife, Sherri, thought this sounded like a fun thing to do, so one morning on our vacation we drove over there.

As we pulled up to the safari entrance, we could see giant deer-like animals walking around by the gate. Just roaming wild. I knew once we entered the facility, I was going to have to call on all my Super Dad strength to protect my family from these wild beasts walking free in the hills of Georgia. That's why I had Sherri drive, so I could be free to control the animals. Because I'm the wild animal expert, right?

After paying the entrance fee, Sherri drove through the front gate, and I noticed one of the workers off to the side filling up bags of food.

"How many bags would you like?" she asked us.

"You mean we can feed the animals?" I asked.

She laughed and said, "Yes. But don't feed any of the horse-like animals. Especially the zebras."

I hate it when someone tells you that you can do something fun, but then they attach a "But don't" to it.

"You can go swimming, but don't get bitten by a shark."

"You can go trick or treating, but don't eat your candy until we get it x-rayed."

"You can test drive this new car, but don't think about buying it."

"You can go swimming, but wait a half hour after eating." (We never go a half hour without food!)

Now "You can feed the animals, but don't feed any of the horse-like ones" had been added to the list of bittersweet freedoms.

After the worker's warning, that's all I could think about. I was looking at every creature as they headed toward our car and was asking myself, *Is that one horselike? How about that one over there?* What I couldn't figure out was, if we weren't supposed to feed the horse-like animals, why hadn't someone told the horse-like animals about this rule? Within minutes we had all sorts of creatures crowding our car, sticking their heads in our windows and looking for food. Our babies in car seats were getting their snacks confiscated by some big hairy thing while I was trying to get out the chart to see who we were allowed to feed and who we weren't. The kids were screaming, there were animal slobbers flying all around, when all of my Super Dad signals began calling me to action.

"Drive!" I told Sherri.

"I can't drive with their heads in the window!"

"Then roll up the windows!"

She tried to operate the windows from her master control, but the animals wouldn't budge. They had no intention of getting their heads out of the way.

As we were trying to shoo them away, I looked up and saw a giraffe standing right in the middle of the road. He was huge! Before long, he, too, had his neck in our car!

Sherri tried her best to inch the car forward while simultaneously keeping an eye on all the backseat commotion. But all she could see through the rearview mirror was giraffe neck.

Up to this point in Big Love's life, he had only seen giraffes either from afar or as a stuffed animal. Now he had the head of one right in his lap, with the giraffe's big old tongue whipping itself all over the car. It had cleaned off the windshield twice, and was starting in on the upholstery.

Wading her way through the giraffe slobbers, Sherri tried once again to reach the window controls. But now a herd of zebras was heading our way. They had little bandanas around their heads and looked like a youth gang. I knew if they reached their destination, we were trapped for sure.

The zebras walked over to my side of the car first. Protectively, I tucked Taz behind me. The zebras tried to stick their heads in the window, but the other animals wouldn't surrender any ground.

Giving up, the Stripes gang walked over to the other side of the vehicle, where a couple of them managed to nuzzle their way through. The sad truth was obvious: word of our junk food had reached every animal in the park, and our car was now one big feeding dish on wheels.

Never in my life did I think that I would be called upon to protect my family from a herd of exotic animals. It hadn't come up in any of my nightmares. It didn't come up in the premarital counseling that Sherri and I had received either. Yet here I was.

"Sherri, you're going to have to put the pedal to the metal and gouge it! You're going to have to just go!"

I guess the animals caught on that we were serious this time, because they all started backing away from the car as Sherri moved forward. We finally got the windows rolled up, almost catching the giraffe's tongue in two of them, but he got it out at the last possible second.

At last, there was glass between us and the safari animals. We were exhausted, but thankful to be alive! There was animal slobber and junk food crumbs all over the car and us. And we weren't a hundred yards into this place. I thought to myself, *what could possibly happen next?*

Just then I looked up and coming over the hill was a herd of yaks. Then Boomer screamed, "Look, Dad, there's an ox!"

I looked in the direction he was pointing and sure enough, a great big ox was heading right toward us, with horns big enough to put a new sun roof on our car. A herd of elk suddenly blocked our way. They wouldn't get out of the road no matter how wildly we tried waving them off. A couple of them even broke out into a fight. Elk road rage.

Even now, my adrenaline rushes as I recount that day. But we made it through. And looking back, I'd have to say it was one of the most exciting days of my life. I suppose in reality we were never in any real danger, and yet the struggle was exhilarating. I'd do it again in a heartbeat.

Come to think of it, feeding all those wild animals was a lot like feeding five kids around the dinner table. The animals were bigger and, in most cases, had a longer reach and a bit more saliva. But one thing's for sure: if you rattle a pack of goldfish snacks and some gummy fruits in front of either a kid or a camel, they'll both rush the minivan.

ON THE HUNT

One day I decided to take a group of my offspring and some of their friends on a deer hunt at the Bubbarosa. That's what we call a spread of woods that Bubba owns that's filled with deer and plenty of other wildlife. It's a hunter's paradise. He built premier shooting houses on the property, and it's perfect for family hunts.

On this particular day I had Taz and Big Love in one of the hunting houses with me. Our friends, Jordie Henson, his son Jordan, and Mark Garnett and his two sons, Hunter and Mitchell, were in the other hunting houses. The weather was perfect. The wind was favorable, which is an important factor in any good deer hunt. We couldn't have asked for better conditions.

Usually when I hunt I don't like to carry a lot of stuff with me. I'm lucky to get there with a gun and a flashlight. But since I had the kids with me, it was a totally different game. I had brought a suitcase full of all sorts of food, drinks, toys, and a rattle bag. Now for all you nonhunters, a rattle bag is something used to attract the deer. It isn't horns. It's a bag of wood that when you shake it, sounds like deer fighting and crunching their antlers together. Deer are territorial. If they think a fight is going on over a female's attention somewhere in their territory, they'll show up as fast as they can. It's like *Desperate Wildlife*.

Up until around four o'clock in the afternoon, I let the kids just kind of goof off. They were standing up and sitting down, playing with their toys, and generally just having a good time. But now it was time to start getting serious. For deer hunters, 4:00 to 5:15 in the afternoon is prime hunting time. It was going to start getting dark after 5:15, and I knew by then our chances of seeing any deer would be pretty much over. So at four o'clock, it was time to stop playing around and get quiet.

Now, mind you, I had already resolved to myself that we weren't going to see anything. The kids were with me; there were far too many variables going against us to have a good hunting day. The noise alone was going to scare off any wildlife. And I was fine with that.

But the kids really wanted to see some deer. So much so that they started making themselves see them everywhere. Taz said, "Daddy! Daddy! I just saw a deer's mouth!"

"What?"

"I just saw a deer's mouth!"

I nodded, like you would do to anyone hallucinating. But he kept going.

"Daddy, I just saw a deer's leg!"

"Okay, but I think he's gone now."

"Daddy! You missed it! I just saw a deer's whole face!"

Big Love, trying to be the older brother, had to chime in. "If you don't be quiet, Daddy's gonna ground you for weeks!"

I told Taz that I wasn't going to ground him, but I would really appreciate it if they'd all just keep quiet for one hour.

But then I got the bright idea that, since the kids were making so much noise, I was going to make a little noise, too. I got out that rattle bag and said, "Guys, watch this. Daddy's gonna make some noise."

I started shaking the rattle bag that sounded like deer antlers colliding into each other. *Kalunk! Kalunk!*

Now they wanted to do it.

"Can I do it, Daddy? Let me do it!"

"I asked first!"

"No, you didn't!"

"Let me do it, Daddy! Let me!"

I got so distracted by them, I wasn't even paying attention to how much I was shaking the bag.

"Ya'll sit down," I said.

I put the bag away, and they changed their chant to:

"Daddy, can we have some snacks?"

"Daddy, can I have another soda?"

"Daddy . . . can I have some of your water?"

As I was handing them a few snacks, I looked out across the field and could not believe what I was seeing. At the corner of the clearing, the far right end of it, there was slight movement. Those of us who have hunted enough can easily recognize that movement as a deer. And any of you who have ever hunted with children know this is also the moment when you start begging your blessings from heaven, promising them anything you can, if they'll only be quiet.

"For the love of all that is good and kind, pllleeeeeeease hush!" I pleaded. "Pllleeeeeeease, pllleeeeeeease, be quiet!"

At this point, you lose your status as an authority figure. You are now a beggar. A whispering beggar, because you don't want to alert the deer of your presence.

"What, Daddy, what?" they said.

I put my finger over my mouth in the "Shush!" position. "Ya'll need to be quiet and put your ear protectors on to muff the sound," I whispered.

It sounded like a good idea at the time, in case I did get a good shot at the deer, but what happened next showed how much I had to learn about kids and hunting.

"I can't get my ear protectors on, Daddy! Daddy, help me! How do you do it?"

I gave them the hush sign again, then helped them with their ear protectors. But now with the protectors on, they couldn't hear how loud they were talking.

"Hey, Daddy!" they shouted. "Have you seen the deer yet?"

"Shush!!!!" I said. I looked out across the field, fully expecting to see the deer's white tail darting away. Even deer can only take so much whining.

But he was still there, peeking his head around the corner. By now, he had to have noticed that there was no fight going on in the field. The only fight was the one in the hunting house. But he didn't move. He just stood there, looking around, checking things out.

I thought about taking a shot, but I knew I couldn't make it. Too bad, too, because I counted and saw that he was at least a six pointer, maybe an eight. But I had kids crawling all over me. Now they were fighting over the binoculars.

"Let me see! Let me see!"

"I wanna see!"

"I had them first!"

"Did not!"

"Did too!"

"Ya'll be quiet!" I begged again. They didn't listen, of course. So it was now time for bribery.

"Who wants a hundred dollars? Toys R Us? Anything you want. JUST BE QUIET!"

The deer finally spotted us. He looked right at me, and I knew if I was going to try to shoot him, this was my chance. He wasn't going to come out any further into the field. His next move was toward the exit. So I told the kids to get back. I picked up my gun, and before I knew it I had that deer in my scope. The kids were still talking, of course.

"Daddy! Daddy!"

"I'm telling!"

"You started it!"

"Did not!"

"Did too!"

KABOOM!

Now, they were quiet.

I did it. Or tried at least. The boys' eyes got real wide.

"You shot?" they said.

I nodded. "Yep, and it was probably straight up in the air."

It's not very easy to hit a target with someone jerking your neck. But now I had their undivided attention.

"Did you get him, Daddy? Did you get him?"

I didn't want to tell them that I got anything because I really didn't think I did. Still, the deer was nowhere in sight, and I hadn't seen him running away laughing at me. So maybe . . . just maybe . . .

I decided to wait a few minutes to see if more deer would come out of the woods. If I missed that one and another one came, I could try again.

But no other deer showed up. So we climbed down out of the hunting house and went to check out the area where the deer might have fallen.

We walked for a bit, but when we rounded the corner and the boys could see the area clearly, their eyes got real big and they started jumping up and down. "You rock, dad! You rock!"

I don't know how I did it with all I had going against me, but there he was. He was a 7-pointer, 140 pounds. I had shot it in the neck, which is a very small area and almost impossible to hit.

It was a long way to drag him back to the car, but we did it.

The hunt didn't make any of the hunting magazines, but it sure made our family album. I was a hero to my kids that day. That's all they could talk about for weeks. That, and . . .

"You're the one who might've made Dad miss that shot 'cause of all your talking!"

"It wasn't me. It was you!"

"Was not!"

"Was too!"

"Was not!"

"Was too!" . . .

Kids. What are you gonna do?

WHY WE LOVE BETTY LOU

To say my wife, Betty Lou, is naive would be putting it mildly. Her innocence is a big reason why I love her. She tries so hard to be one of the team, but sometimes it's as though someone gave her life's rule book in another language, and she's trying her best to fake her way through it. Even under these conditions, she still gives everything her 100 percent.

The following story proves my case.

If you have children, no doubt you've played the game where you trick the kids about what is behind them that they can't see. I play it all the time with our children. Hunter can be sitting on the couch, and I'll look over his shoulder like I'm looking into a chair and say, "Well, I didn't know Paw Paw was here." He knows that I'm messing with him, but I'll just keep on doing it until he can't stand it any longer. When curiosity gets to be too much for him, he has to turn and look. And that's when The Claw gets him. I'll tickle him and he'll try his best to tickle me back, but The Claw is much too fast.

After he has sufficiently screamed for mercy, I will stop. Fathers know instinctively that children need air to breathe. But then, once he makes eye contact with me again, I'll look above him and go, "I didn't know we had a bald eagle nesting in the house." He'll try his best to ignore me, but I'll just keep looking up and say to Betty, "Mama, look at that." Again, he'll try his best not to look. But he can only hold out for so long before finally giving in to temptation. As soon as he does, The Claw gets him again.

On this particular day I was on a roll. I had even gotten down on the floor to make it more convincing. Hunter was sitting on the couch. I looked under the couch and said, "Well, well, I didn't know Sissy (our dog) was under here. Come here, girl, come on."

Hunter tried his best to resist, but I kept on until it was driving him crazy. Finally, he got down with me, looked under the couch himself and started calling Sissy. Quick as a flash, The Claw got him (will he never learn?) and started tickling him again.

All this time, Betty had been watching our little game with the excitement of a benchwarmer at a doubleheader, just waiting for a chance to get up at bat.

She finally got that chance after supper. Hunter was sitting in her lap, and *they were both looking right at the dining room table* when Betty said, "Look, Hunter, there's Paw Paw sitting at the table." Are you getting this scene? Both of them were staring straight at the table, and Betty said, "Look, Hunter, there's Paw Paw."

Hunter, who was two-and-a-half years old at the time, leaned away from his mother and looked up at her like "That's not how the game is played, Mother. I was looking at the table. You're supposed to make me look at something else and then get me to turn around. What you're playing is called 'hallucinations.'"

Being the caring, understanding husband that I am, and not wanting to embarrass my lovely wife, I said, "Betty, what are you doing?"

At that moment, she must have realized what she had done, and she started laughing at herself. Like I said, though, it wasn't her fault—the rule book that she was handed wasn't in her native tongue.

I assured her the whole matter would be our family secret. Then I called Rick. He's like family. I also talked about the incident on our radio show. Our fans are like family. And now it's in this book. (If you paid your hard-earned money for this book, you're considered family, too.)

But after this, the story is going into the vault, never to be mentioned again.

Like I said, though, Betty's innocence is a big part of why I love her so much. Moments like that are precious. This is a woman who has a college degree in nursing, and at one time administered drugs to people for a living. And yet, as one of our radio guests so aptly put it, "You can almost see Betty saying to a little kid in the pediatrics ward, 'Honey, this isn't gonna hurt a bit.' Then she sticks the needle in her own arm."

I told Betty that she could add her own comments here, but she's too busy trying to convince me that my editor's at the front door, even though the door's open and I'm looking right at it.

As they say in the South, Bless her heart.

HOSTAGES

Screened-in porches are big here in the South. They're a place where you can sit and enjoy the beautiful outdoors without fear of mosquitoes swooping down and airlifting you to another state.

When I was growing up, none of the houses I lived in had a screened-in porch. So when we built our new house, I wanted one. I like how screened-in porches become a gathering place for everyone. There's just something about them that says, "Sit down and stay a while."

Our screened-in porch is almost like a big bird cage. That's the shape of it. It's kind of round and can seat quite a few people, plus one cat. Our cat likes our screened-in porch a little more than it should, so it's had to be punted out of there a few times. (Just for the record, no animal was harmed in the writing of the last sentence. *Punted* is probably a poor choice of words, anyway. It's more like tossed, like an ice skater would toss his partner into the air with the full confidence that the partner is going to land on her feet and continue on her way. Only we weren't on ice and neither one of us ice skates.)

But back to my story.

On this particular weekend, the humidity was down, and we had a houseful of company. So Sherri and I decided that we should move everyone out to the screened-in porch and pass the rest of the afternoon out there, eating ice cream and drinking tall glasses of sweet iced tea.

It was the perfect way to spend the afternoon. The kids were playing off in the corner, and all the adults were visiting and having a great time.

Right in the middle of it all, I noticed Big Love get up and go back into the house through the back door. Now, mind you, this is the only door back into the house, and for that matter, the only way off of the porch, period. I watched as he went into the house and shut the door behind him. I was a little curious as to why he was going back into the house, so I looked up and asked Sherri, "Where's he going?"

"Oh, he's probably just going back in to get a toy or something," she said.

Sherri was probably right, but at that moment my father's intuition and a sinking feeling came over me. I had caught a glimpse of him fiddling with the lock as he was shutting the door.

"I don't know how to tell you all this," I said to everyone. "But I think Big Love just locked the door."

No one paid much attention to what I was saying. They were too engrossed in their own conversations to care about my tattling on a five-year-old. But I knew what I had just seen. And I wasn't a tattle-teller. I was a professional radio personality who would soon have to be leaving for a sound check for a concert later that night. If Big Love had just locked us all out of the house, there were going to be some significant problems. How would the event planner explain my absence to the audience? That Rick's five-year-old had locked him out of the house, so he couldn't show up? Sure, the story was believable, but I had been paid a retainer. I had to show up, or I would have to give the money back. And it was too late to repossess everyone's lunch.

"Boomer," I said. "Go over there and check that door and see if your brother locked it."

Boomer got up, walked over to the door and checked it. "It's locked, Dad," he said, unconcerned, and then returned to doing what teenagers do best—eating.

I wasn't panicking yet, but I was beginning to grow a little uneasy. I could see Big Love making his way to the kitchen. Unsupervised kitchen access where everything is at your disposal and no one is around to tell you that you can't have this or you can't eat that, this was a five-year-old's dream. Heck, this was *my* dream. I knew Big Love was about to pass the point of no return. If he reached the kitchen and realized that nothing and no one was standing between him and the stash of junk food, he was never going to open the door for his family again.

But, like I said, I was trying not to panic. I was just hanging out with everyone, all the while keeping sight of Big Love out of the corner of my eye. I was also watching the clock tick away, closer and closer to the time I needed to leave for my sound check.

Then the inevitable happened. Big Love had reached the kitchen. Now he was in the process of moving the little stepstool over to the counter, no doubt so he could climb up and start rummaging through the cupboards for Cheetos and Fruit Loops. He glanced in my direction, and I'm pretty sure I saw him smirk when he caught me looking.

I thought to myself, *Why, you little . . .*

But I stopped myself short. I didn't finish the sentence or say it aloud because I knew that one day I'm going to have to give account for every word that comes out of my mouth.

Anyway, as a parent, your first reaction in a situation like this is, "Hey, as soon as I get my hands on you . . . !" But where would an outburst like that get me? The game was on, and a five-year-old boy with Cheetos-orange fingers held the power. If I scared him, he was never going to let us off the porch. I had to try a different approach.

"Son . . . I sure do love you, buddy. Hey, I'll tell you what, why don't you come over here and open this door and let us all off the porch?"

Big Love appeared to think about it. Just as he reached for the Oreos, he seemed to hesitate just a bit, as if he was going to come to our rescue. But then he froze. It was as though he suddenly realized that no matter how much his daddy was smiling now, once Dad came in where he was, he was doomed. Instinctively Big Love had to know that locking your family out on the screened-in porch while you pig out on junk food might be off the charts on the disobedience scale. He had to have known that no matter how gentle my voice was or how convincing that smile on my face was, his goose was cooked. No wonder he wasn't about to open that door!

I looked around for some moral support, but no one else seemed to be all that concerned. My parents weren't expressing much worry. It was as if they'd been through this same sort of thing before with their own offspring. I doubted it. Like I said, we never had a screened-in porch when I was growing up. Still, there they sat relaxed and kicked back, just waiting for the problem to somehow resolve itself.

I decided to try one of the windows that led from the patio into the house. Maybe one of us could go through a window, I suggested aloud, then regretted it as soon as I did. I'll tell you why. One of the things I get furious about at my house is the fact that Sherri will not keep those windows locked. In fact, just fifteen minutes before this incident happened, I had talked to Sherri again about this problem. We have double windows, and I had shown her how you push up the window first, then you push it down, and then you lock it. I explained how when she doesn't lock it, we are just letting air in and throwing our hard-earned money away. Of all days, Sherri had picked this particular day to listen to me and had locked all the windows. So now, while I was busy trying the windows, Sherri was saying, "Well, normally, I'd just go over and open the window that I always keep unlocked, and we'd be in the house already."

She was clearly initiating the *I Told You So* play, but my defensive line was ready.

"I'm still right on that," I said as firmly as any man locked out of his house by his five-year-old son could. "You shouldn't leave windows unlocked."

I briefly considered the possibility of going out through one of the deck windows, but that was about a ten- to fifteen-foot drop down to the ground. We clearly had no good options. We were stuck between a rock and a Big Love.

Meanwhile, Big Love was inside eating cookies and crackers and whatever else he could get his hands on, without the slightest fear of adult intervention. Every once in a while, he would lick his fingers and take a quick glance over in our direction. Not a total look of defiance, but as close to it as a five-year-old could get. Probably more along the line of ornery.

I knew if I didn't do something quick, he would eat us out of house and home. So I tried a little bribery.

"Hey, Buddy," I said. "Hey, Little Man, Daddy loves you. I think there are some M&M's up there on the top of that shelf. Right over there. Yeah, that one. If you let me come in, I'll get you some."

Now, all of a sudden the family appears to be paying attention. They haven't reached my degree of panic yet, but they're all talked out and ready to get off the porch and into some air-conditioning. Sensing our combined plight, they've now become my backup. Cheers of "That's good, that's good" hail my M&M tactic.

It wasn't until he took the stool and moved it over toward the top shelf that I started to move from irritation to concern. I was concerned that he might get hurt, of course. And I was also concerned about something else: My five-year-old was moving a stool over to the counter to see if I was telling the truth. The little son of a gun was checking up on me!

I gave him a look as if to say, "How do you think this is gonna end, son? Do you really think you can take over the house like this? Do you honestly believe that you can stage a coup and keep your parents, the people who birthed you, the people who love you, out on the porch forever?"

To be honest, I kept waffling between wanting to wring Big Love's neck and admiring his ingenuity. Not that he planned for all of us to be out on the patio at the same time or thought the whole thing out ahead of time, but the way it had worked out, with him alone in the house with all the snack food—you have to admit, it was pretty creative.

So I kept shifing from, "Hey, Buddy, Daddy loves you," "Hey, why don't we pick out a movie and watch it together," "Wanna bring Daddy a cookie?" to "If I get my hands on you, you little . . ."

Again, I didn't finish that sentence. But this was a hostage situation for sure, and we needed a negotiator brought in. Someone who could talk Big Love out of the house, or at least talk him into letting his family back into the house.

I tried virtually everything to get him to let us in. I asked Sherri to sweet talk him. I even got his brothers to try to coax him out. Taz gave it a try, and then Boomer. Brandi would have tried, too, but she was away registering for school. As a last resort, I brought in the grandparents as a sympathy play. The whole Burgess bunch was standing at the window, posed like a family portrait and smiling with our faces pressed against the glass.

"Look at your family, Son," I said. "We're all trapped out here on the porch. Why don't you let us in now, Son? Seriously. Come on, Buddy, I need you to let us in. I'm starting to really mean that . . . a lot." But the kid didn't budge. Now I'm thinking, I'm going to have to break a window. He's locked us out on the screened-in porch and I'm going to have to break a window to get into my own house. That'll mean I'll need to call a glass repair man, and then I'll have to explain the whole story to him. Not only were Big Love's actions going to hurt my career if I didn't show up for the appearance that night, but now they were going to cost me the price of a new window—and possibly, my reputation as a man, a mature adult in charge of his own destiny. But my five-year-old wasn't playing fair!

I was back to "If I get my hands on that little . . ."

That time I almost finished the sentence. But at last he started to come around. He strolled up to the window, and we started talking through it. Well, I was talking. His mouth was crammed full of cookie pieces.

"Hey, Big Love. Give me a little sugar," I said, hoping he would open the door in an attempt to give me a kiss, and I'd be able to grab it before he could shut it again. But the kid didn't fall for it. I knew I was close, though. So I kept talking to him through the window hoping something would work.

Taz was even losing his patience now. He walked over to the door and started beating on it. I guess that's what finally got through to Big Love because for some reason he suddenly decided that he'd had enough solitude (and sugar), and at long last he opened the door for us. I was so relieved I wanted to hug him! Right after a good scolding! What he did was dangerous. He could have gotten hurt. Or worse—we could have all starved to death out there on the patio! We had only been locked in for about fifteen minutes, but our ice cream and iced teas were long gone, and a few of us were beginning to show signs of dehydration. I think I even lost a pound or two. But I did manage to make it to my sound check.

It took us three paydays to restock the cupboards with everything Big Love had eaten. And now, whenever we spend the afternoon out on the screened-in patio, I always make sure we leave the house windows unlocked—and Big Love in plain sight at all times.

THE RICK & BUBBA CODE
TO UNDERSTANDING FAMILY

I have an interesting family. My brother Greg, who has been a guest on our radio show numerous times, has his own unique take on life and politics.

For one thing, he doesn't believe in second-term inaugural parties. "Why are we doing that again?" he'll ask. "Can't we just say, 'You know that oath you took four years ago? It still stands.'"

Greg is passionate about things that no one else thinks about. One of his missions in life is to stop puppet-to-human interaction. This sort of thing drives him insane. He literally hates it. He's fine with puppet-to-puppet interaction. For example, growing up he was fine with *The Muppet Show*—that is, until the guest stars showed up. He just couldn't stand the idea of live people interacting with the puppets. The old television show *Alf* just about drove him over the edge.

Nowadays, Greg has to deal with computer-generated characters mingling with human actors. He'll lay awake nights wondering why they couldn't have found a Great Dane and trained him to play Scooby Doo in the movie. Why did they have to go with animation? How many Great Danes were out there just waiting for their agent to call? But they gave the part to a computer-animated dog instead and thus sent my brother into such a depression that he didn't eat for days.

Greg also hates song medleys. Not because you never get to hear the whole song. He hates medleys because of the face that the band members make every time they transition to a new song.

Movie sequels? Hates them, too. He almost got into a fight once with a guy who thought that *Lethal Weapon 2* was better than the original.

Greg even has a problem with military bands. "Why do we have a trained killer playing the tuba?" he'll ask.

I'm sure you won't be surprised to learn that he believes in conspiracy theories too. Not all of them, but some. Like the one about doctors and pharmaceutical companies being in cahoots. He almost died once because he refused to go pick up his prescription. He said he was trying to outsmart his doctor. "That's how they get you," were the last words he managed to say just before passing out.

Child prodigies are something else Greg doesn't buy. No child, he claims, wants to sing Broadway tunes. He thinks that parents should be able to acknowledge that a kid's got talent without having her sing *Swanee*.

It's not just my brother. My mother has a few quirks, too. I love her, but she has a Master's Degree in guilt. In fact, I believe she was valedictorian of her class.

She also has a habit of telling those "Mom lies."

"Mom, what do you want to eat?" I'll ask.

"Oh, Honey, it doesn't matter."

"Okay, how 'bout fish?"

"Oh, I don't want fish."

Why don't moms just say that it really *does* matter? She knows exactly what she wants to eat. But she'll let you go down through the list until you get to it.

When I first got voicemail, my mom thought it was a sign that I was getting too big for my britches.

"Mr. Big Pants got voicemail" is the message she would leave every time she got my recording instead of me. To her, my getting voicemail was akin to going on *The Apprentice*.

And I love her diet plan. She'll point out that I've put on a few pounds and need to go on a diet. Then in the same breath, she'll ask, "Is something wrong with the food I made tonight? Because I noticed you didn't go back for seconds."

If I ever forget to visit, she takes it like most other moms. She went in for knee surgery once, and I forgot to call. I tried to apologize, but she just said, "You don't forget about the people you love." She acted like it was some kind of test. She wouldn't even let my siblings call to remind me. "Rick has to remember this on his own," she'd say.

I didn't remember it, of course, and thus moved down in the offspring rankings to #4 on her list.

She only has three children.

Mom loves being "in the loop." But she needs to be. She's the information agent of the family. A mother's gossip is the best. Have you noticed how all mothers, regardless of race, financial standing, or religion, always start sharing news with the same words, "Now, I don't want to say anything . . ." which in mom-speak means, "Get ready for some juicy gossip."

Growing up, we could always count on mom being an equal opportunity disciplinarian. In our house, everybody got spanked. At home, in public, it didn't make any difference. She'd even spank other people's children. That was the way it was back then. The whole neighborhood raised you. If you did something wrong, complete strangers would spank you. "If your momma only knew what you did!" they'd say; then they'd swat you across the backside. Everybody was in on your discipline. When a bunch of us did something stupid like setting the woods on fire, my dad took care of the discipline for all the other families. For weeks other parents were coming up to my dad and saying, "Coach, thanks for keeping the kids in line." You couldn't do that today.

My father was very competitive. A normal dad would let his kid win every once in a while. Not my dad. If he were to let us win, that would mean he'd have to lose, and losing just wasn't an option for my father— even if it was to a four-year-old. Hunting was where he was the most competitive. He would spend all day teaching us how to shoot, getting us all hyped up, and then at the first sign of wildlife he would shoot at it before any of us could even draw a bead on it. Then he'd make us drag it back to the car.

Even if he never let me win, I remember thinking my dad was the bravest man I knew. He was raised around animals, and I'd often see him catch possums and other wild animals with his bare hands. He seemed fearless to me. And even though he could be hard, I always felt secure and knew beyond any doubt that he loved me.

Dad had a few quirks, too. He would drive a truck way beyond the time anyone should; and once, when we needed an air conditioner in our house, he just cut a square out of our wall and stuck the air conditioner in the hole. Not in a window. Right into the wall.

His biggest quirk surrounds something that—thankfully—hasn't happened yet. It has to do with his final request.

My father has told me that when the time comes that he doesn't have his full faculties operating, when some of the rides have shut down like at an amusement park, rather than going off to a nursing home, he wants us to take him out to the place where he likes to hunt and leave him there in the woods. I am not kidding about this. I wouldn't kid about this. My dad wants to be dropped off in the woods to finish out his life there. He says he doesn't want our last memories of him to be visiting a rest home every Sunday afternoon and feeding him lime Jell-O.

He wants to spend his final days with his rifle by his side. Most rest homes frown on this, preferring that patients just push the "Nurse" button instead. Not only does my father want his gun by his side, he wants to maintain a little mystery about himself in his final days. He wants to become a legend around his community, where people will say, "Have you seen that old long-haired man who runs through the woods around here?"

My father's dream is to be like Big Foot, only in jeans and a football jersey. You may be laughing, but he's already shown me the spot where he wants me to drop him off. He wants to hunt for his own food and live off the bounty of the land, and of course, get his social security check. He's figured out a way to do that, too. There will be a mailbox out on the road near the woods, and every first of the month he'll come out and pick up his check.

My father has thought a lot about this. He says he'll kill wild animals and eat them, then use their carcasses for clothing. He wants to exist like this until he just fades away into the sunset one day, never to be seen or heard from again. His legend will continue, however, and like all legends, it will become more and more exaggerated through the years.

I'm not saying that we should actually fulfill this last wish of my father. I'm just saying that this is what he has requested. You have no idea what my brother and sister and I go through. We know that this is his final desire, but how can we carry something like this off? I don't think they let you just drop off a loved one in the woods like that. Elderly people have wandered into the woods on their own and had to be rescued, but they weren't dropped there. You probably would go to jail for something like that, even if it is your father's dying wish. He has made out a living will, but I don't know if he included an Abandonment clause in it.

And what about the owner of the land where he wants to be dropped off? Whoever owns it might not want a legend just wandering around on his property. My father's answer to this is, "Nobody asked Tarzan whose land he was on. Do the other wild animals in the woods have to get permission to come onto someone's property? Of course not. They just roam free."

If we do manage to pull it off, Dad has already planned out a visitation plan. He said I could go back and check on him at a pre-arranged time and place (probably by the mailbox where he'll be picking up his social security checks), and he'll come out from the woods and meet me. I'm to sit there with the grandkids and wait, and when he's sure the coast is clear (no tourists with cameras trying to get a picture of the legend for supermarket tabloids), he'll come out and talk to us. The grandkids might not recognize him with his long hair and beard, and he may have resorted to animal-like mannerisms by then, but he'll still be Grandpa.

HOME ALONE . . .
WITH DAD

Since we host a morning radio show, both of us are blessed to be able to spend a lot of time with our children. This is a wonderful thing. Most of the time.

One morning I was on the telephone with singer/songwriter Jerry Reed of Nashville. Because it was a land line, I couldn't leave the room to go check on the kids who were playing in another area of the house. It was like being back in the 1960s, before cell phones. I could hear my heirs and none of them seemed to be in any trauma, so I figured everything was fine and went ahead with my telephone conversation. After a while, though, it seemed like the baby's voice was sounding farther and farther away. I wondered why. Was he some sort of ventriloquist prodigy who could throw his voice at such an early age? Or could something be amiss once again at the Burgess compound? I hung up and went to go check on things.

When I walked into the room where the boys were playing, I couldn't believe the scene before me. There they were, playing a board game and getting along amazingly well. They were moving their game pieces around the board so politely I thought I had somehow been beamed into the wrong house. If memory serves me correctly, I think I even heard a "please" and two "thank-you's." It would have looked just like a Norman Rockwell painting had it not been for one tiny little problem. *The baby was nowhere in sight!*

"Where's the baby?" I asked, not really alarmed—more curiously concerned at this point. But I knew since Sherri had left the children in my charge, "I know where most of them are" was not what she wanted to hear when she returned. So I repeated,

"Where's the baby?"

I knew they had heard me. Probably both times. But when engrossed in a board game, it's hard sometimes to avert your attention to something else . . . like the whereabouts of your baby brother!

Again, I wasn't panicking yet. In fact, I was sort of comforted by their lack of concern. It can't be anything bad because they're not worried, right?

"Where's the baby?" I said, and this time they knew I wanted an answer.

Without taking their eyes off the board game, they simply shrugged and said, "Outside," and continued playing.

"Outside?"

They nodded.

"How'd he get outside by himself? He can't open the door."

I looked outside and sure enough, the baby was out there. Just him . . . and the dog. The dog was licking food off his face, but other than that, he appeared to be safe.

Apparently, what had happened (it all came out in the Burgess Family Inquistion that followed) was the baby kept interfering with their board game, and so they did the only thing they could do. They removed him from the temptation. They opened the back door and placed him out there and sat him down far enough away that it would take a while before he could make it back to the porch. Somehow it made perfect sense to them.

It was not going to make sense to their mother, and I was sure to get the blame. At a moment like this you don't really care about parenting or handing out punishment. You just don't want your wife to find out. You need a plan not to get caught. Most of my mess-ups I can explain away to Sherri. After so many years of marriage to me, she's come to expect certain disasters. But this one was going to be a little more difficult. What were those kids thinking? Didn't they realize that when I'm not paying attention to details they have to be, or we're all up a creek when Momma comes home?

I ran out into the yard, shooed the dog away, and rescued the baby.

Then I scolded his two siblings for what they did. It's irresponsible to put your brother outside when your dad who was supposed to be watching him is busy talking on the phone. Where was their sense of duty? They need to learn to pay attention to what's going on around them and not just focus on their own little world. They should have put down that phone—I mean board game—and given the baby the attention he needed.

When Sherri got home and asked, "How was everything?" I told her the only thing I could tell her.

"Fine. Oh, and you don't have to worry. The baby has already had his bath."

THE RICK & BUBBA CODE TO BABYSITTING FOR DADS

Women have been passing down their mothering secrets to each other for years. They know it's a good thing when the younger generation can learn from the mistakes of the older generation. We think us dads should be helping each other in this same way, too. If we can save just one father from slipping up and learning a childcare rule the hard way, then our lives will have had purpose.

With this thought in mind, we now offer the following Babysitting Rules to all you Super Dads out there. Read and learn:

1. Try to stay in the best possible shape. Remember, even if they're only two years old, it's still a matter of survival of the fittest.

2. Pouting and whining is not acceptable behavior and should be dealt with promptly. If your wife lets you get away with it, you'll only set a bad example for the kids.

3. It is perfectly normal for you as the caretaking parent to have repeated nightmares about purple dinosaurs.

4. Dad will want to check in with Mom every so often on her cell phone to make sure she doesn't come home and surprise Dad while he's watching the game on TV and is unsure of where the children are.

5. Band-aids will solve almost any injury.

6. If Dad is sleeping, the following rules apply:
   A. Do not throw ball near Dad's head or any other body parts.
   B. Big kids watch little kids.
   C. In case of injury, refer to Rule #5.
   D. No loud noises. This includes explosions.

7. No matter how cute he or she happens to look in it, spaghetti is not proper headwear.

8. Children under the age of ten are not old enough to cut their own (or their sibling's or pet's) hair. This includes shaving, too.

9. Bedtime is eight o'clock. No exceptions. If the kids won't let you get to bed by that time, then do the mature thing: when Mom gets home, tattle on them.

10. Any disasters that happen when Dad is in charge stay between the kids and Dad, and of course whatever emergency personnel or insurance adjusters were involved.

It's not easy being a dad, but in defense of fathers, we do have to say that there has been a disturbing trend in America in recent years to push the idea that dads aren't all that important in a child's life. Nothing could be further from the truth. Children need their fathers. And they need their mothers to respect their fathers. Do dads make mistakes? Of course they do. Do moms make mistakes? Of course they do. Are we dads sometimes afraid of our responsibilities? Absolutely. Are moms sometimes afraid of their responsibilities? No doubt about it. Do dads sometimes look inept? Yes. Do moms sometimes look inept? Yes. Parenting is a "learn as you go" process, and even the best parents will admit to making their share of mistakes along the way.

Someday we're all going to look back over the parenting we did, and we'll find things we're proud of and things we wish we had done differently. But hopefully, if you're a dad, the one thing you'll be most proud of is that you stayed involved in your child's life. No matter what. If you're not involved in your child's life now, get involved. The good news is, it's never too late to be a Super Dad.

PART VI

DECODING RICK & BUBBA

What is the origin of Stonehenge?

Who is the mastermind behind the pyramids?

Why do things disappear in the Bermuda Triangle?

What makes Rick and Bubba tick and why in the world are they so popular?

Mysteries. The answers are beyond our human knowledge. And yet, Stonehenge exists. The pyramids still stand. More luggage gets lost in the Bermuda Triangle than anywhere else on earth. And the Rick and Bubba phenomenon continues to astound even the brightest minds. The world longs for understanding. Maybe this will help . . .

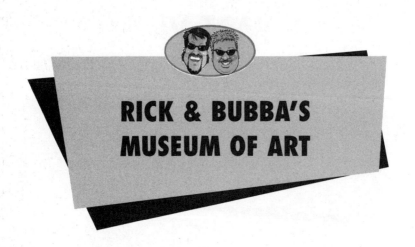

RICK & BUBBA'S
MUSEUM OF ART

Like in *The DaVinci Code*, art plays a central role in *The Rick and Bubba Code*, too. And much of this art can be found at the Rick and Bubba Radio Station and Museum of Art in Birmingham, Alabama. Here is just a small sampling of some of the masterworks that can be found there:

The Big Boy statue—No, it's not Michelangelo's *David*, but it's hard to deny that there is an uncanny resemblance. The only difference we can find is that our statue is wearing more clothes. Put a pair of checkered overalls on the *David* statue, and all those European tourists would start craving a double cheeseburger and chocolate shake before they knew what hit them.

The French Fried Potato Eaters—similar to Van Gogh's most famous painting, *The Potato Eaters*. But ours is just a little bit greasier.

Elvis on Velvet—we've tried donating this museum quality piece to the Louvre, but they keep returning it. Obviously they don't think they can afford it. It's all right, though. Our financial advisors tell us that this one piece of art could be our retirement.

And, the two most important paintings of all—*The Rick and Bubba Self-portraits*. If they bear a slight resemblance to Brad Pitt and Tom Cruise, it's merely a little creative license. It's our heads on their bodies. But in the interest of conservation, we had to do that.

We only had just so much paint.

SNAKES IN THE LINE

I don't like snakes in any way, shape, form, or fashion.

I have made no secret of this. Anyone who knows me, anyone who has heard our radio show knows this one fact about Bill "Bubba" Bussey—I do not like snakes! I did not see the movie *Snakes on a Plane*. I did not see *Anaconda*. I did see *Indiana Jones and the Raiders of the Lost Ark,* but I remained under my seat and did not buy any black licorice.

Whenever I see a snake, even if it is safely put away in a cage, I will go into a near-hypnotic state. Once again, I'm like Mowgli in *The Jungle Book*. (I really liked that movie.) My eyes start spinning, my head gets woozy, and I am no longer in control of my actions. I cannot knowingly be in the same room, or area, or even the same state for that matter, with a snake. I don't like big snakes, small ones, poisonous ones, nonpoisonous ones, friendly ones, ones that only eat other snakes, not even rubber ones.

I cannot be around snakes, no way, no how, no sir. I become a different person around a snake and absolve myself of all responsibility. Those who have witnessed my actions while I'm in the presence of a snake say I quite literally go berserk. Rick has seen me in this state on several occasions and can attest that it is not a pretty sight.

The worst incidence of this transformation occurred some years ago in

Alabama. (Note: For those of you who may be a little on the squeamish side, I warn you now that this tale involves death. You might want to skip to the end of the chapter. For the rest of you who feel my pain, read on.)

Here's how it all went down. There is this one area in Alabama where Rick and I have on numerous occasions done "remotes" for our radio show. A "remote" is when you go on location and do the show from another city or state. This particular place was a nice community, and the people there are very friendly. The only bad thing is that the fans there like to bring their animals out to meet us.

Now, for the record, we certainly don't mind meeting house pets—dogs, cats, hamsters, that sort of thing—because it does make the crowd look bigger. But these people don't have regular house pets. These folks bring their cougars, pigs, cows, ostriches; we've had all kinds of things show up. Most of the animals do listen to the show, though, so even they're okay with us.

On this one particular day, however, we were standing in the parking lot, doing our show and meeting people, shaking hands and signing autographs, when a lady came up to us holding a bag in her hand. Now for all I knew, she could have been shopping. I wasn't thinking anything at all about the bag. She waited through the line and finally got up to us. She said, "Well, I just thought I'd bring my pet to show you." And with that she reached into the bag, whipped out a snake, and stuck it in my face.

Did I mention I don't like snakes?

I don't remember how big that snake was, but I want to say about forty feet. It was probably more like three. All I know is when I came back to my senses, I was standing there frozen in what appeared to be a Kung Fu-like position. At my feet, a lady was laying on the ground, crying over what apparently was her now dead snake. I looked at Rick, whose eyes were as big as softballs, for some sort of explanation to the scene I saw before me. But he didn't respond. He just stood there with his mouth gaping open.

"Rick," I said. "What just happened here?"

I had no clue what had happened. I really didn't. All I knew was I had been meeting the fine people of this community, and their animals, when all of a sudden I blacked out. Everything else was a blur.

"Well" . . . ." Rick said. "It seems you jumped into the air with all the grace of Bruce Lee and kickboxed that poor woman right in the chest."

"No, I didn't."

"I'm afraid you did."

"Why in the world would I do that?" I asked, trying hard to bring my memory into focus, but still convinced that he was joking.

"I'm not sure, but she went flying into the air, did two somersaults almost in a continual motion, and now she's lying there on the pavement crying."

"But she's holding a limp snake," I said, thinking perhaps I had just heroically put a stop to some sort of satanic ritual.

"It was her pet. She was trying to show it to you when you picked that poor snake up by the head and began to beat it against the pavement."

"No, I didn't," I said.

"After about the fifth blow, the head finally came off of it and you let it go. Then you bowed for applause and assumed the defensive Bruce Lee position again."

Now Rick has been known to pull a good prank on me every now and then. But that was before we both signed a treaty against practical jokes. Besides, I knew in my gut that the carnage around me could not have been a practical joke. I couldn't deny what I was seeing: There was a lady on the ground holding her chest. She was also holding her head where she had apparently hit the pavement. And she was clutching a dead snake in her hand, crying real tears. I was sure there had to have been another explanation for what I was seeing, but at the moment I couldn't come up with one.

I was certain that I hadn't kicked her, but I couldn't deny that I had done something to the snake. Whatever I did, to the snake or to the lady, my defense was solid. I wasn't in my right mind. I was Mowgli. I was in a snake-eye induced trance. I wasn't in control of my actions. On top of that, I had just eaten a Twinkie and was in the throes of a sugar rush.

For the record, I am truly sorry for whatever happened, and for the demise of that poor woman's pet snake, but my motives were pure. I'd be happy to send her a replacement snake, but like I said, I hate snakes. If I'm responsible, though, I will try to make it up to her somehow.

And for those of you who might be contemplating standing in a Rick and Bubba autograph line in the future, let me just say you have nothing to fear. Rick and I don't make a habit of kicking our fans in the chest. I'm not saying it won't ever happen again, especially if one of you whips a snake out of a bag, but it is for the most part an unusual occurrence.

RICK GETS HIS DUE, BUBBA GETS HIS FRANKFURTER

I understand that officials at my old alma mater, Oxford High School in Alabama, are finally catching Burgess Jersey Fever and have begun looking into the possibility of having my football jersey retired. For you nonsports fans, this is a lot different than a wife just wanting an old shirt retired. This is an honor, for any sports figure.

Trey Halliday, the new principal at the school and a fellow teammate for the all-state high school football game we played back in '83, told me that he is doing whatever he can to get the appropriate approvals. He has already dusted off my Golden Helmet Award and moved it to a more prominent spot in the trophy case. "That's step one," he assures me.

I always felt down deep in my heart that my old high school would do something like this for me. I knew they loved me. That's why they kept me there for so many years. I loved Oxford. I tell everyone about Oxford. It's the exact halfway mark between Birmingham and Atlanta, so if you're ever driving to one of those cities, stop in at my old high school for a pit stop. And tell them Rick sent you. You can also drop a hint about them retiring my old football jersey. (I've got to do whatever I can to pump up enthusiasm for this cause.)

I realize it didn't help that while I was at college, Troy State, I became a troublemaker, disappeared, and joined a rock band. But I was trying to find myself. I still am. That's why I stay this size. It's to make the process a lot easier.

Nor did it help when I walked off the field during that one high school football game. But I had to use the restroom. And then there were all those times that I dodged the workouts. While the rest of the team was running around the stadium, I hid in a hole that had been knocked out of the brick wall. Then when the team got close to the finish line, I would climb out and join them like I had been running the entire time. To pull that off required impeccable timing and skill. No wonder they're even contemplating retiring my jersey. It's either for my athletic accomplishments, or they just don't want to see my number on the field ever again.

I think the possibility of this honor has made Bubba a little jealous, though. He's starting to work now on getting his high school to do something in his honor. So far, the only department that's answered his calls is the cafeteria. They're thinking of having a hot dog named after him. It's not a team jersey like he deserves. But still, the Bubba Bratwurst does have a nice ring to it.

DEATH BY TIGER

I live by the code, "Never have a pet that can take you."

I don't want to go for a walk in my backyard and have to worry about some pet of mine jumping on me from behind and tearing me to shreds. I have two Golden Retrievers and a Cavalier King Charles spaniel, and I can take all three of them at once with one hand tied behind my back. That's how it should be.

I don't understand why anyone would want to keep a pet around their house that could potentially kill them. Why would someone want boa constrictors, pit bulls that have tasted human blood, tarantulas, and all sorts of other exotic animals that could easily take them down while sharing the sofa with them? What are these people thinking? Why would they put themselves in this kind of jeopardy?

Without a doubt the worst way to go would be to be eaten by some animal. That's not how I want to go. Don't get me wrong. I would put up a good fight. In fact, if it's ever on the news that Rick Burgess was killed by an animal, when the facts of the case are divulged, two things will be clear: 1) it must have been a surprise attack and 2) I fought to the death. Witnesses will say, "Man, poor Rick went nuts on that animal!"

"Who could have foreseen that a Siberian tiger would climb through his open bedroom window (even though, as we all know, he repeatedly told Sherri to lock them) and attack him from behind just as he stepped out of the shower?"

But our fans love Sherri and won't blame her for the unfortunate incident. They will understand that during Alabama's hot, humid summer, you have to open your windows if you're not running the air-conditioning. It's the law. What you don't expect, however, is for a tiger to come jumping through one of them. So when the news of the attack breaks, everyone will know that I could not have possibly seen it coming. I was simply caught off guard, with no possible means of escape.

"Rick put up quite a fight," Sherri will tell our family and friends in her e-mail blast. (Individual phone calls would take too long, and with e-mail she can attach photos.)

"Rick is gone," her announcement will begin. "But he fought back nobly. He was no match for that big cat. Still, the tiger knew he wasn't messing with just any ordinary human being. When they pulled Rick's lifeless body out from under the mangled animal, you should have seen the clumps of tiger hair that Rick still had clutched in his hands. There was even a piece of tiger ear in his mouth. My brave husband gave it everything he had."

I'm not bragging here. I just know that no matter what kind of wild animal attacks me, I will rise to the occasion. I will not go down without a fight.

That is a promise to all of you.

Other Unthinkable Scenarios for which I've Prepared Myself

The scenarios that I've stayed up nights preparing myself for are as endless as they are varied and furry:

"It beats all I ever saw. That poor Rick Burgess had just stepped into the souvenir shop when a charging rhino followed him in and attacked him right there by the turquoise jewelry. There was no way he could have seen it coming."

Or . . .

"I tell you what, ol' Rick was just sitting in his car at the drive-through getting ready to announce his order when that bear got out of line and came up to his car and attacked him right through his open window. Somehow he mustered up enough strength to drive on and pick up his order, but he died shortly thereafter. It breaks my heart. Poor Rick . . . even seasoned french fries couldn't save him this time."

And then there's this one . . .

"Rick Burgess was on the field working out with the kids on his football team when what appeared to be a rabid leopard leaped at him from his blind side and attacked him in his 3-piont stance, right there by the 40-yard-line. Who would have thought something like that could happen right here in Birmingham? They say the critter didn't have a single spot left by the time Rick got through with him."

Or the heartbreaking yet poignant . . .

"The Burgess annual lake outing turned tragic when the family hero and patriarch, Rick, attempted a triple back flip off the rope swing, only to land in the jaws of a Great White Shark. Marine biologists are still puzzled how the sea creature could have ended up in Oxford Lake."

"With his head deep into the shark's jaws, Rick did the only thing he could. He reached his arms up and poked that big fish squarely in the eyes, like Moe would do to Curly, then he socked the critter to kingdom come. Unfortunately, four more sharks were waiting in the wings (again, how they got into Oxford Lake is beyond us), and poor Rick ran out of steam around number three. The only time he came up for air was when he said, 'Start heating up the skillet,' but he was never seen again."

I realize the odds of any of these things actually happening are ridiculously small. I would take comfort in that fact but for one thing: the odds of a lot of what happens to me in life are ridiculously small. Needless to say, however I leave this world, know this— I am not going down without a fight.

Even if I have to take half the rain forest with me!

THE RICK & BUBBA CODE—
THE MOVIE

When *The Rick and Bubba Code* movie comes out, we want all of our lifelong fans, as well as any of you who may be getting acquainted with us for the first time through this book, to know that we have made a pact between ourselves that under no circumstances will we allow worldwide fame to go to our heads. We have seen this happen in far too many overnight success stories and do not want to fall into that ego trap.

That having been said, we see no harm in being prepared for the inevitable. Therefore, we have been picking out our dressing trailers and practicing signing our autographs more quickly. So far, the trailer that we like best is a two-story double wide, with a satellite hook-up and a big screen TV. We think we're also going to demand our own personal chef and have already decided to hold out for someone from the Waffle House.

To prepare ourselves for the media blitz, we have been conducting mock interviews. We want to be prepared for all those tough interview questions like whether it's true that Penelope Cruz secretly wishes we were single. This, of course, is ridiculous. She knows we're both happily married. She's just going to have to lower her sights and wait for the second best to come along.

We've also been thinking about which megastars they should cast to play us in the movie. It's not an easy choice, but if we were to go strictly by looks and stature, I would like to see Mel Gibson play me in the movie. Rick sees Tommy Lee Jones in his role with Robert Duvall as a back up. Jack Nicholson's name has also been tossed into the mix.

That would be our dream cast. But once budget concerns kick in (after all, nobody in Alabama has any money left after chipping in for the presidential fund-raiser and our new football coach, and the food budget on this film is going to need to be tripled if Rick and I are going to be around daily as consultants), the casting director will probably go with Jim Belushi and Kevin James. They're both fine actors and would do a great job. But by not casting Mel, Jack, Robert, or Tommy, the show will be missing the whole physical similarity thing. The director may decide to do it that way, but the audience is going to have to suspend reality and use their imaginations more than they would otherwise. But it's out of our hands.

Some of you who have followed our careers know that this won't be our first movie experience. Rick and I had speaking roles in a movie called *Rustin*. We had one line each. Our agent didn't want to run the risk of over-exposure.

PART VII

DECODING THE SOUTH

Life in the South is a little different than it is in other parts of the country, or the world for that matter. We have our own system of doing things down here. If you're planning a trip to the South, it would be a good idea to study up on the culture before you go. Just like any foreign country—France, Italy, Los Angeles—the South has its own language, its own customs, its own way of looking at life. Here's Lesson One of Rick and Bubba's Guide to the South:

When you travel south of the Mason-Dixon line, it helps to do a little research, too. Watching the recent film version of *The Dukes of Hazzard* won't help you, either. Daisy's accent was purely contrived.

No, if you want to fit in down in the land of Dixie you need some education from people who know how to make iced tea. You can choose to forego it and plunge in cold turkey; but we'd bet our country ham that, though the people you meet will be polite and even friendly, they will be sure to say this one meaning-filled phrase about you when you go, "Well, bless your heart."

THE RICK & BUBBA CODE TO THE SOUTH

Following is just a small sampling of some of the information that can be found in our Secret Code to the South:

Cicadas

The South has cicadas. Lots of them. They're harmless to humans, and if you stand outside on a late summer afternoon, you can hear them loud and clear. It sounds like a concert of crickets on steroids. It's an eerie sound that goes straight through you, and it can make the hair on the back of your neck stand up. Some Southerners (no one we know personally) actually eat cicadas. We're not sure how they're prepared, but most likely they're fried. Cicadas look a lot like locusts, but rumor is they taste like chicken.

Humidity

You know you're living in the Deep South when you are unfazed by a grown man standing there talking to you without a shirt on. We Southerners understand humidity and know that it can sit on you like a wool jacket on a summer day.

You'll do anything to cool off, including removing pieces of clothing that in arid settings, would stay on. Perhaps our native humidity is why all true Southerners use ice in their drinks, and are baffled by those who don't. It's just not right.

The upside to our climate is that we get to know what it feels like to be a dinner roll.

Slower Pace

No one is in a hurry in the South. We don't want you to be either. If you're ever told that you only have a year to live, we would highly suggest that you move to the South. It will make your time seem like twice that long.

In the South, every move you make has to be thoroughly thought out first. Every syllable of every word has to be drawn out. We live life in slo-mo. And we like it like that.

Socializing

It doesn't matter if you're celebrating or grieving, food will always be involved. In Los Angeles, it's "Let's grab some coffee." In the South, it's "Let's have a potluck." We don't believe that you can carry on a conversation without plenty of food around. Here, cornbread brings more people together than Dr. Phil.

Mosquitoes

We have mosquitoes so big they've been known to escort girls at halftime during our football homecoming festivities. Enough said.

Southern Hospitality

Yes, it really does exist. People from all parts of the globe who have traveled to the South comment on our good ol' Southern hospitality. Southern people really are that friendly. In other parts of the world, you have to prove yourself worthy to be a friend. In the South, you start out as a friend and will remain a friend until you do something to mess it up. Don't misunderstand. There are things that you can do to lose this "friend" status. For example, saying something stupid like you don't know who "Bear" Bryant is. (For those of you who don't know, Paul "Bear" Bryant was the best college football coach of all time. Being in the South and not knowing this is worthy of a flogging.)

Another thing you should know about Southern hospitality is that we just naturally assume it goes both ways. In other words, if you say something hospitable to us, we will take your word for it. We don't understand empty promises. If you say "Drop in and see us sometime," we will.

I (Rick) have thought of surprising our house guests some time when they're in the driveway about to leave. I'll wait for them to say something like, "Why don't you guys just come on and go home with us," and I'll answer, "Okay!" Then I'll grab our eight pieces of packed luggage from behind the bushes and yell, "Quick, kids! Get in their car!"

If you're going to say something to a Southerner, you'd better mean it!

Speaking Southern

Hawaii has "Aloha." The South has "Bless your heart." Though at times used as a type of verbal salve after a bit of potent gossip, a well-timed "Bless your heart" can make everything seem okay.

Another thing about the Southern language is total strangers will ask you, "How's your momma?" They have no idea whether your momma is even alive; but if they run into you, they will inquire, "How's your momma?" They won't ask "How's your dad?" I guess they don't much care about him. But they will never let you go without asking, "How's your momma?"

We could write an entire book on all the various slang and catchwords of the area, but we don't have that much ink. You'll just have to come on down and experience it for yourself. Bless your heart.

Football

Football is just different in the South. For one thing, we don't tolerate losing. Other parts of the country can accept a loss. We can't. We're behind our team as long as they're winning their games. But if they ever start to lose, we'll turn on them.

We should also mention that in the South, we enjoy the major leagues, but it's the high school and college games that truly capture our attention and loyalty. Only in the South will you find people willing to fight for a college they didn't even attend.

SOUTHERN LABELS

We're not sure why, but it seems that the rest of the country feels compelled to label certain things "Southern." Like if a comic is from the south, he or she will be labeled a Southern comedian. Jeff Foxworthy, Larry the Cable Guy, and too many others to name are often billed as "Southern comedians." But do you hear Jerry Seinfeld or Jay Leno being referred to as New York comics? When's the last time you heard a comedian introduced on national television as a Nebraskan comic? But Southern comics get labeled as soon as they open their mouth—the accent, you know.

We both have been told that our radio show would be carried in more markets if we didn't sound so "Southern." We try to explain that the reason we talk like we're from Alabama is because we are from Alabama. Look, if a joke is funny, we don't care if the person telling it is from down South, up North, back East, or beyond the moon. We're going to laugh.

Once, Sherri and I (Rick) took a vacation to Martha's Vineyard and you wouldn't believe how fast word spread around the island that there were Southerners in their midst. Not just Southerners. Conservative Southerners. Not just conservative Southerners. Evangelical conservative Southerners.

The islanders were going around cautiously eyeing every stranger and saying, "Are you the ones?" When they finally did find us, and visited with us a bit, I think they liked us. But then what's not to like about an evangelical conservative Southerner? Most of us are just friendly, hard-working, patriotic, God-fearing people who love family get-togethers with lots of food. And by the way, how's your momma?

BIKER BISTRO

One look at our size and most people take our restaurant recommendations seriously; which is good because, not to brag, but we do seem to have a sixth sense for finding good eating places. Once in a while, though, even we miss.

Like the time when I was in the Blue Mountain Beach area of Florida with my family. I was trying to find a restaurant to accommodate our party of eight. It was a very busy time of the year, and we wanted to get away from the crowds and just have a nice, quiet meal. My search led me to what I thought was the perfect seafood restaurant.

Now, mind you I had a wife who was in her third trimester of pregnancy with only about six or seven weeks to go. Her hormones were raging, and finding a restaurant for someone in that condition wouldn't have been easy even under the best of circumstances. We also had the Killer Bee's (Taz and Big Love, ages six and four) with us.

I should pause here and offer a warning to any of you who may run into us out in public sometime: My wife and I do our best to discipline our children, but they do seem to have a knack for finding trouble wherever they go. They've been solely responsible for the early retirement of far too many waiters, child care workers, and Chuck E. Cheese employees. Should you run into us in public, consider yourselves duly warned.

Now on this particular night I had also invited my Sunday school teacher and church deacon, Mark Garnett, and his wife to join us, along with their two children.

After my sales pitch, the Garnetts agreed to give this new restaurant a try. Both Mark and I figured if it was a seafood restaurant, they had to at least have a good shrimp basket. We set the time we were to meet in front of the restaurant and spent the rest of the afternoon salivating over what fried and fishy ecstasy awaited us.

That night, my wife and I arrived at the restaurant about five minutes before the Garnetts. The restaurant was nothing like what we had imagined. As soon as we pulled up in front of it, Sherri said, "Rick, what have you done?"

I wanted to answer her, but I was speechless, which as most of you know, doesn't happen too often. Even I couldn't defend my choice of restaurants this time. All along the front of the restaurant, dozens of motorcycles were lined up in a row. The building itself wasn't much more than a shack with neon signs announcing beer and a live band.

Suddenly, it dawned on me that I had just arranged for my family and our Sunday school teacher's family to have dinner together at a Florida biker bar. I was pretty sure this was covered somewhere in the Bible.

Needing a little time to come up with an alternative plan, I pulled our family van onto the gravel parking lot and parked between a couple of Harleys. There was a tattooed man with a parrot on his shoulder hanging around by the front entrance. That's not something you see at Denny's, so I figured he was either the bouncer or the health inspector. Either way, it was beginning to look like it was going to be a long night for both the parrot and us.

Sherri didn't want to go in at all. I believe the words she used were, "We are NOT going in, Rick!" (Did I mention she was pregnant?) I told her that we were probably jumping to conclusions. For all we knew this was a very good restaurant. Besides, we couldn't leave before the rest of our party arrived.

It took some convincing, but I finally got Sherri to agree that we'd get out of the car and go on inside to check it out while we waited for our friends.

We made our way up the ramp, past the tattooed man and on to the front entrance. Before opening the door I told our kids that under no circumstance were any of them to say a negative word about Bachman-Turner Overdrive or the Doobie Brothers. "If you don't like whatever music is being played inside, keep it to yourself!"

As we opened the door, I fully expected to see Patrick Swayze and Sam Elliott standing there checking IDs, like in the movie *Road House*. But no one was checking IDs. We just walked right in. It took a while for our eyes to get adjusted to the darkened, smoke-filled room, but finally (and unfortunately) they did. It was a rough-looking crowd. Sometimes it's better not to know the danger you're in. Every person I could see could easily take me. They were huge. I had never seen so much leather, metal chains, full body tattoos, and body piercing in my life. And that was just the women.

I had already planned to ask for the nonsmoking section, but now I wondered if I should settle for the nonkilling section.

No one even acknowledged our existence. They just kept playing pool. So there we stood—my pregnant wife, my kids, and me, putting our lives on the line for a good shrimp basket. In other words, life as usual for the Burgess crew.

Finally, I heard a voice yell out from the midst of the smoke, "Just go on back. There are some tables back there."

I wasn't sure who the voice belonged to, but since it sounded pretty big, I decided we should follow his directions.

We walked to the back and found a table all set up. There were eight chairs around it, just as our reservations had requested. We were far enough away from the bar area now, so we felt a little more comfortable. This was obviously the restaurant portion of the building. Granted, they had to move the deejay booth, and we had to help them roll a band amplifier out of the way; but at least we were seated.

I felt I should warn our Sunday school teacher and his family about the ambiance they were about to step into. So I called them on their cell phone.

"Hey, Lynn?" I said.

I had gotten his wife. That's good, I thought. Maybe she would be more understanding. Moms usually understand mess-ups.

"Yes?" she said.

"I'm going to ask you a very straight question here. Do you have a problem with eating at a biker bar?"

The pause that followed was even more pregnant than my wife, Sherri. Then the Sunday school teacher came on the phone. "Oh, we're here already, Rick. And first of all, let me commend you on your courage for going in that place. Where are you at? We can't see you for all the smoke. Did they have a fire?"

"We're actually at a table. In the back," I told him.

"Did you see the guy with the parrot?" he asked.

"Yes, as a matter of fact, the kids are playing with the parrot right now."

I had taken some creative license there. Big Love wasn't actually "playing" with the parrot. He was talking to a man with a cockatoo who was talking to the guy with the parrot. I wasn't sure, but from a distance it looked like both birds had tattoos, too.

While we were still on the phone, I looked up and saw the Garnetts making their way toward us. We greeted each other, and after everyone took their seats, we started making guesses on when we thought the first fight was going to break out.

We could have left, I suppose, but by then all I could think about was the shrimp basket. I told our little party that they could sit there and be upset at the guy who recommended this restaurant (that would be me), or we could all appreciate the fact that these folks had a table all set up for us and we would be eating, hopefully, a delicious meal very shortly.

Every other restaurant in town had a long waiting list, so the consensus was to stay and give this one a try. We placed our orders and were just starting to relax when I looked around the room and noticed that Big Love was missing! I looked under the table, under the chairs, and behind the amplifier. He was nowhere to be found. But I knew he couldn't have gotten far—I had just talked to him a few seconds earlier. There were only a few logical possibilities. Maybe he

a) Went to the bathroom, which he never should have done alone, and he was going to hear about it from me if that's where he went.
b) Was hiding under the table, which he knows got him into big trouble the last time he pulled that.

c) Was over by the pool table "playing pool" with some very scary
   looking individuals.

If you answered "c," you'd be driving home in your new car right now
if I had been offering prizes. Not only was Big Love over by the pool table,
but he had just picked up the 8-ball from off the table and was now playing
keep away with it. The tattooed people weren't laughing.

It's kind of funny, but when you're in a situation like that where you
feel like your life may be in imminent danger, you find yourself thinking
things like, *Well, I've still got four children.* "Son, I love you, but I did tell
you not to get out of your seat, didn't I? There is a plus side to your future,
though, Son. You'll grow up to handle a Harley Davidson like nobody else.
And don't worry, I'm sure they'll let you write to us."

I quickly put those thoughts out of my head as my fatherly instinct
kicked in, and I realized that even if I had to lay down my life or a couple
of vital organs, I would do whatever it took to rescue my offspring.

I eased my way toward the pool table. The tattooed people were
snarling. Reaching for Big Love I said, "Gentlemen, I apologize for my
son. Here's your ball back. If you want to start over, just go ahead and rack
'em back up."

The tattooed people didn't blink. In fact, I don't think I've ever seen
anyone go that long between blinks. While I continued to try to convince
them of my sincerity, Big Love was taking the pool chalk and dropping it
in all the pool table holes because he thought it was funny.

"Hey, little fella," I said. "Why don't you come over here by Daddy.
Come on. Walk over slowly. Don't make any sudden moves now," I said,
figuring that they wouldn't dare hit me if I had my kid standing in front of
me. This is a ploy that has always seemed to work for me.

Except this time. They started moving toward us. I grabbed Big Love
by the hand and the two of us started walking, more like running, in the
direction of our table. Naturally, no one in my party was paying all that
much attention. They were too busy talking about the guy who made the
reservations at this restaurant. Garnett had some idea that I might have gotten myself into some kind of a situation just by the fact that that's what I

do. But even so, he was just sitting at the table saying, "The shrimp basket should be here any minute." Neither he, nor anyone else, had my back.

Big Love and I remained focused on our survival. All we had to do was somehow make it back to our table safely, finish our meal, and get out of there as quickly as possible. The tattooed people would start another game of pool, and all would be right with the world.

But I hadn't counted on the tomato. What tomato, you ask? The one I didn't see on the floor and ended up taking a ride on. Suddenly, my feet slid out from under me, and I flew into the air. I then came crashing back down in the middle of a sea of tattoos and metal chains.

Garnett, who up until now had been primarily focused on the where-abouts of his shrimp basket, saw me and figured whatever situation I was in had just escalated, and I was now being beaten up by a bunch of guys with cue sticks. To his eye, it seemed like they were wailing on me, and I needed backup. He got up from the table, but before he actually threw in and made the biggest mistake of both of our lives, I managed to crawl over and tell him about the tomato.

He breathed a sigh of relief that could be heard two counties over. If you don't have to come to the defense of a good friend in a biker bar, it's usually a welcomed thing.

Other than all that, I'd have to say it turned out to be a pretty good restaurant and evening. I don't think we'll go there again, though.

No shrimp basket is worth your life. But it did come close.

DON'T GIVE ME ANY LIP

Before I begin this story, I must tell you that I have pets. I love pets. But if you have a pet and it stays in the house with you, you might want to pay close attention.

Apparently, one day the police in Warner Robins, Georgia, received a call about a family pet who had chewed off a woman's bottom lip while she was sleeping. I guess I should say "allegedly chewed off the lip" in case the dog has retained legal counsel.

I have called the investigating detective and have verified that the incident did indeed take place. I will attempt to treat this sad tale with the respect it deserves and refrain from making comments like "I guess she was all out of Kibbles and Lips."

According to the police, criminal charges will not be filed against the pooch at this time. This was a first offense for the one-year-old canine. The dog's forty-seven-year-old owner doesn't believe the dog did this on purpose. In the past she would often let "Shorty," the poodle perpetrator, lick her lips after she drank sweet tea. The dog got accustomed to this activity and apparently got hooked on the refreshing Southern beverage. Southerners can understand this. Sweet tea is addictive. For the few who may not know, sweet tea is simply tea that has enough added sugar to be officially classified as a dessert.

When the woman fell asleep that day, Shorty alledgedly began licking the sweet tea off of the woman's bottom lip as he had done many times before, but this time the pooch got a little carried away and chewed the lip right off her face. This could have been his way of asking for a refill, but we're not sure.

The most amazing thing to me is that the woman remained asleep through all of this. The police report said that she had been taking a pre-scribed pain medication which may have been a contributing factor.

It seems this wasn't the only time Shorty had gotten carried away, though. On another occasion, again while she was sleeping, Shorty man-aged to take her false teeth right out of her mouth and chewed them all up.

I'm not a dog psychiatrist, but it would seem to me that Shorty has some boundary issues. Whether the false teeth tasted like sweet tea or whether he was just trying to see how he looked in them, again I can't say. Whatever Shorty's motives in both situations, the obvious action, in my opinion, seems to be some kind of intervention.

Thankfully, doctors were able to perform several surgeries to recon-struct the victim's lip, using skin from elsewhere on her body.

So where does this leave Shorty? The victim says that she is going to keep the lip-eating poodle. She can't whistle for him anymore, but one thing you can say about this woman is that she sure is loyal to her dog. And that's not just lip service either.

PART VIII

DECODING RELIGION

Faith is important to both of our lives. Aside from the spiritual gratification, there are a lot of other good things to be gained from going to church. Without an active church life, we'd have a lot less material to work with. Let's face it, a lot of funny things happen in church. And for the most part, Christians have a great sense of humor and will help you hone your comedy. The problems come when some people think that those in the pew are supposed to be perfect. But we've got it all wrong. The pew isn't a trophy shelf for saints. It's a gurney for sinners. Some of us have forgotten that along the way.

THE RICK & BUBBA CODE
TO THE GOOD BOOK

It amazes us how little some people know about the Holy Bible. One morning a lady called in to our radio show and when asked this question, "According to the Book of John, Peter said to Jesus, "Thou shalt never wash *what?*" She answered, "His broom."

We are not making that up. Now for the record, we have both read the Bible from cover to cover numerous times, and we can't recall it ever referring to the disciples having a broom. I'm not sure which translation that woman was using. Perhaps it was the Martha Stewart version. As far as we know, neither the disciples nor Jesus owned a broom. Needless to say, she didn't win.

Because of answers like this, we've started a Know the Good Book campaign. Our goal is to educate people on what the Bible says, and more importantly, what it doesn't say.

With that in mind, we provide the following pop quiz:

1. God parted the Red Sea for this man. Was it . . .
   a) Ezekiel
   b) Charlton Heston
   c) Moses
   d) Earl

2. When God called Jonah to go preach to the city of Nineveh, he . . .
    a) Immediately obeyed God's calling and went there.
    b) Marched around Jericho seven times.
    c) Ran from God and boarded a ship to Tarshish instead.
    d) Said, "I'm going to Disneyland!"

3. When God told Noah to build an ark, Noah . .
    a) Put up a patio instead.
    b) Wrote to HGTV to request a nautical makeover.
    c) Obeyed God and built the ark, whereupon his life and his family's were saved.
    d) Said he'd get to it later. The Super Bowl was on.

4. Daniel spent the night in the lion's den because . . .
    a) All the regular bed and breakfasts were booked.
    b) He was helping his son with his biology project.
    c) He refused to stop praying to God.
    d) He had signed up for Adopt-a-Pet.

5. Lot's wife turned to a pillar of salt because . . .
    a) She obviously had not been sticking to her sodium-free diet.
    b) You can never have enough condiments.
    c) She disobeyed God and turned back to look at the destruction of Sodom.
    d) Sodom was already on fire, so who needed pepper?

6. Joseph's brothers hated his coat of many colors because . . .
    a) He was always leaving it around the house.
    b) They were allergic to it.
    c) They were jealous.
    d) It was so 2500 BC

7. In one of Jesus' parables, he told of two men who each built a house. One man built his house on a rock, and when the storm came, that house stood. The other man built his house . .

a) On the lake, got a fishing boat, and was rarely seen at home again.

b) At the end of a nice cul-de-sac.

c) On the sand and when the storm came, it crumbled and fell.

d) In California and lost his shirt when the housing market crumbled.

8. In the Book of Revelation, the Bible tells us that the rapture of the church will take place . . .

a) Pre-tribulation.

b) Post-tribulation.

c) In a twinkling of an eye.

d) During a Southern Gospel Quartet Convention, and afterward it will rain toupees for twenty minutes.

9. Esau sold his birthright to his brother Jacob for . . .

a) His CD collection.

b) A copy of his term paper.

c) A bowl of stew.

d) A turn to ride shotgun on the family camel.

10. If you read the Bible every day, you will . . .

a) Have no problems.

b) Have no questions.

c) Gain peace, grow closer to God, and know the answers to quizzes like this.

d) Miss a lot of TV shows.

*Give yourself 1 point for each "c" answer. If you scored 10, it's obvious you haven't been sleeping in church.

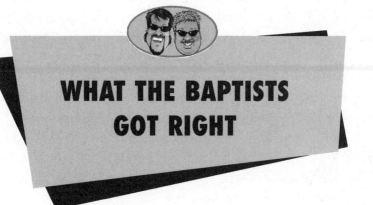

WHAT THE BAPTISTS GOT RIGHT

Before you jump to any conclusions, we want to say that this isn't going to be a chapter debating the difference of doctrine between the many Christian denominations in the world. They all have their pluses and minuses. Even our denomination, Baptists. We're both Baptists, but we've been around long enough to realize that even Baptists aren't perfect.

Still, there are certain undeniable areas where Baptists just "get it right." One thing is the length of the pastor's sermon. Baptist ministers understand they have to have the sermon wrapped up in twenty minutes if their congregation is ever going to beat the Methodists to the buffet. (They never have to worry about the charismatics. They won't get there until half past two.) Getting to the buffet is also the main reason that so many Baptists sit on the back row at church. It's so they'll have quicker access to the exit doors and thus to the parking lot.

I (Bubba) will start having uncontrollable stomach growling after twelve o'clock. If the sermon goes beyond that, the preacher's voice must compete with what sounds like a lion loose in the sanctuary. By 12:30, I need help walking. I feel guilty and embarrassed about all of this; after all, Jesus fasted forty days, I should at least be able to make it through one sermon. But it's all out of my control. There is absolutely nothing that a person can do to keep his stomach from growling, other than feeding it. A burp you can control. Other bodily noises you have a certain degree of power over, or at least a warning so you can make a quick exit. But the stomach has free will and growls with no warning whatsoever. Everyone will turn and look at you, once they determine that the sound they heard wasn't thunder, and there's nothing you can do but try to sing all the louder. This singing and growling can be disruptive if it's during the sermon.

So when it comes to matters of food and faith, the Baptists get it right. There does seem to be a direct correlation between food and faith in the Bible. The Bible is full of meals. And they're not snacks either. They're feasts! The feeding of the five thousand (the world's first all-you-can-eat fish fry), manna from heaven, Jesus turning the water into wine, Jesus filling the fishing nets to overflowing, the Marriage Supper of the Lamb in heaven—the list goes on and on.

Even after Jesus rose from the dead, He appeared to His disciples and showed them his hands and feet to prove it was Him. But because of their joy and amazement, the Bible says they couldn't believe it was really Jesus. He asked, "Do you have anything here to eat?" Then they knew it was Him.

Later, when Peter and some of the disciples had spent the night fishing but hadn't caught anything, they woke up the next morning and saw Jesus standing on the shore. They didn't realize it was Him this time either. Again, He asked them if they had anything to eat. They said no. Jesus told them to cast their nets on the right side of the ship. They did and drew up at least a year's supply of sushi. Another food miracle! It *had* to be Jesus. Excited, Peter and the others rushed to shore and found that Jesus had already made a fire and was cooking breakfast for them! Even for Peter, the disciple who had denied Him three times.

When we look at how many times Jesus made sure that there was plenty for everyone to eat, we wonder if food might have been a running joke among the disciples. "What's for dinner?" "I don't know. Ask Jesus." We're firmly convinced that Jesus had a healthy sense of humor. Just look at some of the exchanges He had with the legalistic Pharisees. He was the master of comebacks. When Jesus was seen having dinner at Matthew's house with some people of ill repute, the Pharisees threw a hissy fit about what kind of example He was setting. Jesus asked them, "Who needs a doctor? The sick or the healthy?" Then He went back to eating.

Following His example, we too are of the belief that food is an integral part of church life. It may be the number one reason that we've both felt drawn to the Baptist denomination. We're sure other denominations appreciate a good after-church dinner on the grounds, but Baptists just seem to do it better. At least that's been our experience. But now if any of you Methodists or Presbyterians would like to invite us over for a taste test, feel free to write to us. When it comes to this sort of thing, our prayer has always been, "We'll go where you want us to go, dear Lord."

PEW PET PEEVES

The following are just a few of our pet peeves of church life. They're nothing to make us lose our religion over. But at times these things do get on our nerves. So since this is our book, we thought we'd mention a few.

1. Don't sing "I've Got the Joy, Joy, Joy, Joy Down in my Heart" if you've got the "Scowl, Scowl, Scowl, Scowl Up on Your Face." Believers should be the happiest people on earth because of the hope we have in Jesus. So why are many of us grouchy?

2. Don't start a building program unless you need a new building. My (Bubba) father used to always say, "Have you ever noticed how the guy who stands up and says 'We need a new building' is never there when it comes time to pay for it?'" Too many church splits happen during a building program. Don't build a church to add members if you divide it in half in the process.

3. Why do we build a basketball gym and then call it something like "Abundant Life Center"? Why can't we just call it what it is, a basketball court? The court might even be a good outreach if the neighborhood knew it was available and that they could get to know some of the church members while shooting hoops on a Saturday night. They might even come back on Sunday to check out the service.

4. If you're a businessperson, don't play the "Christian card" early in your sales pitch. Unfortunately, it's almost a guarantee that salespeople who do that are probably going to do something to you or your checkbook that you're going to have to forgive them for.

5. If you're going to claim Christ in what you do, make sure what you do has merit. If we want influence in music, movies, and television, then we need to produce projects that are better than what is already out there. Let's not just complain and boycott. Let's provide good alternatives. Don't just gripe about the pie being burned. Go whip up some banana pudding!

KEEPING THE FAITH

Our friend, evangelist Rick Ousley, once said, "Football is a great game, but it makes a lousy god." We love football, but we're smart enough to know that what Rick Ousley said is true. In fact, the same thing can be said about a lot of things in life—our jobs, our bank accounts, our political leanings, celebrities, french fries, just to name a few.

Faith is an important part of who we are. We both openly share our faith on our radio program, and in our books. We don't do it because we're adamant about putting it in, but because we couldn't in good conscience leave it out. We simply can't talk about our lives without including this very vital part of it. From getting the kids ready for church on Sunday mornings to the way we view our future, our faith is integrated in all we say and do. We may fall short at times, but that doesn't mean God has ever fallen short on His end.

Because of our openness with our faith, people often ask us if we have received much criticism over it. Our answer always surprises them. We tell them, "Yes, sometimes we do get criticized, but you would be shocked if you knew who it was coming from in the majority of the situations."

Our criticisms haven't been from those outside the church. The unchurched seem to be fine with us sharing our faith. Whatever criticism we have received has come, sadly, from other Christians. They'll say things like "You shouldn't be laughing about that," or "You should be more somber and more spiritual."

They may have a point. Or they may not. But we do know one thing—our job is to entertain. To get people to laugh, and if the opportunity arises, we feel very comfortable in sharing the reason behind our joy.

God knows our hearts. We wouldn't want to offend anyone on purpose. That's just not who we are. But we do like to laugh. If you've ever listened to our radio show you would know that we almost always laugh at ourselves first.

Besides self-deprecating humor, we also laugh at our denomination. We say things like "Where two or more Baptists are gathered, there will be a covered dish." That's funny, and it's true. The best humor comes from truth. Covered dishes are a part of church life. If you think otherwise, then you're obviously a visitor.

Don't get us wrong. We always want to take God seriously. But ourselves? We humans have to laugh at ourselves because there are just too many things about us that are funny. And that includes Christians, too.

A person, no matter how cranky, would be hard pressed to find scripture that condemns joy. In fact, there are plenty of scriptures that point to the fact that God is the giver of joy. Joy is the believer's best calling card.

And so is peace.

And unconditional love.

Someone once took a survey that asked people what they really wanted in life. Do you know what the number one answer was? It was peace. Not wealth, not power, not youth, and not even the perfect body. Just peace. To be able to lay their heads down on the pillow at night and rest securely. To not have to worry about bills, broken relationships, hurting loved ones, wars, terrorist attacks, a stock market crash, or anything else that might keep them up at night.

Jesus promised us that if we live the life He talked about, we would have peace. John 16:33 says, "I told you these things, so that in me you may have peace. In this world you will have trouble. But take heart! I have overcome the world!"

Did you catch that one line? "In this world you will have trouble." Not *if* you have trouble. It says you *will* have trouble. And problems. And disappointments. And pain. Life just seems to come with all of that. It's not an option. It's just part of the package. Yet it is in the midst of these storms that we can be assured that God is with us. Somehow, someway, at some point in time we will see that everything has turned out for our good. Our "Why me, Lord?" may be answered here in this life, or we may have to wait until we get to heaven for our answer. But someday we'll see just how the whole puzzle has fit together.

If our words have revealed anything to you, we hope that it is this: There is a God, He has a Son, and that Son died and rose again so that if you believe in Him, you can have the gift of eternal life. It not a secret code hidden in some ancient painting. It's written in the Bible. And it's right in plain sight.

PART IX

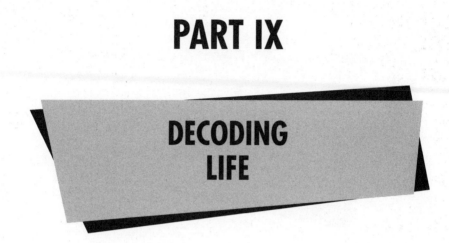

**DECODING
LIFE**

For thousands of years, people have been searching for the hidden secrets of life. Where can they find happiness? How can they avoid stress? Why can't they button the same buttons they easily buttoned just two weeks ago? Life presents us with a lot of questions, doesn't it? In this section, we are going to do our best to answer some of life's questions for you . . . if we know the answers. If we don't, we'll answer them anyway because, well, we have a book to finish.

WHISTLE WHILE YOU WORK

Whatever happened to the idea of people being happy in their jobs? And why is it I seem to get all the unhappy people waiting on me?

I seem to remember an old motto that goes like this: "The customer is always right." But the attitude I usually find myself running into today whenever I need help is, "What do you want me to do about it?"

I once witnessed a man ordering a hot dog at a hot dog stand.

After he placed his order, the girl disappeared into the back for what seemed like forever. When she finally reappeared she said,

"Sorry, we can't sell you a hot dog."

"Why not?" the man asked.

"They're not ready."

Did I mention that this was a *hot dog* stand? How did a hot dog stand get caught off guard by a guy ordering a hot dog?

"What do you mean they're not ready?" he asked.

"There aren't any on the grill. You don't want us to give you a cold one, do you?"

Watching the teenager's mind work through this dilemma was like watching a lava lamp. Only there's usually a lot more movement going on in a lava lamp.

"You want something else?" she asked.

"No, I just wanted a hot dog. I guess you can just go ahead and give my money back," the man said, disappointed.

It was at this moment the frustration turned into the ridiculous.

The girl looked him right in the eye and said, "You got a receipt?"

I am not making this up. If this had happened to me, I probably would've gotten myself arrested. This girl was the same person who had just taken his money for the hot dog. She knew he had ordered the hot dog and paid for it. *And now she wanted his receipt?*

The man finally did get his money back, but I don't think the clerk ever "got it." Lately, it seems more and more people who are supposed to be providing a service to us just don't "get it." It's like we're somehow bothering them if we ask them to do what they're being paid to do. Don't get me wrong. The majority of service professionals are still good, hard-working people. But there does seem to be a growing number of the other kind. If you, too, have encountered some of the "other kind," then the following, recently discovered Rick and Bubba's Code for Understanding Service Professional Lingo will help you. It blows the cover right off all the secret rituals of some service professionals and lets the common man in on the truth behind some of their empty promises and excuses.

THE RICK & BUBBA CODE FOR UNDERSTANDING SERVICE PROFESSIONAL LINGO

Disclaimer: The following does not in any way apply to all service professionals. Only the ones we tend to run into on more occasions than we'd like to think about.

> **Service Professional line:** *How may I help you?*
> **Secret meaning:** "Please don't ask me to do anything that will require any form of thought, work, or energy on my part."

Some of the worst clerks, in our opinion, are the ones you encounter, or rather don't encounter, at some of these home improvement mega stores. We won't name names here, but at one certain place, when you can even find a clerk, his or her answer to your question will always be the same: "That's not my department." You could walk up to a guy standing there wearing a paint-covered apron, mixing a can of paint, and wearing a company vest that says "Stan, Paint Department," and if you ask him a question about paint, he will answer, "That's not my department."

And is it just us or have you also noticed that when you're walking down an aisle at a super store, if you turn quickly, you can sometimes catch just a glimpse of someone who looks an awful lot like an employee ducking into the next aisle, seemingly trying to avoid you? It's like catching a glimpse of Big Foot, only in the Big Foot video footage, he seems to be walking at a much faster clip than that service professional you think you just saw.

The main problem with some of these super stores is that they make them as big as a small city. Not only do you need a map to find your way around, but while I was in a super store the other day, they were holding their own mayoral election.

And why is it that there may be twenty-six check-out stations in these stores, but only three of them will be working? No matter how crowded the store is, or how long the check-out lines have grown, they won't open up another station for anything. They don't even open the extra stations at Christmastime.

After months of undercover investigation, we think we've figured out why so many of the checkout stands sit idle. The reason is—we were shocked to find this out ourselves—all the other stations are fake. Remember when bands used to have an entire wall of amplifiers but only three of them would actually work? All the rest of them were phony. It's the same with these check-out stations. Those cash registers are hollow. They're illusions. The store owners just want us to think there are twenty-six check-out stations so we'll hold onto the hope that another lane might open while we're waiting one hour and forty-seven minutes to buy a box of nails.

Why don't they just be honest with us? Why don't they post a sign over their entrance that says, "When you cross over this threshold, you are on your own." Who among us wouldn't appreciate that kind of honesty? It's better than being duped into believing that the nice guy mixing paint in a paint-covered apron that says, "Stan, Paint Department" might actually know a little something about paint.

Service Professional line: *Your call is important to us. Please continue to hold, and we'll be with you as soon as possible.*

Secret meaning: Your call is a pain in the neck to us. Please hang up and don't ever call here again.

Let's face it—if our call was so important to them, why would they be putting us on hold? If it's so important, why are they making us listen to

Paul Anka music? The least they could do is give us the Beatles. Or something palatable. Anything except an orchestration of Inagaddadavida. Or any kind of Muzak.

Hey, here's a suggestion from a radio guy. If they're going to insist on putting us on hold, why don't they take song requests? Why not let us callers pick which song we want to listen to while we wait for them to get around to answering our phone call? Personally, I (Rick) wouldn't mind hanging on the line if I knew I could listen to "Free Bird." (Unless it was played on an accordion.)

This is probably a good time to also bring up the fact that never in the history of the world has a person called a complaint line and not heard the words, "Our regular business hours are. . . ." Whenever you need to call a complaint line, even if it's right in the middle of a working day, you will never hear a live voice. It's just the rules of complaint lines. You can't fight it.

Service professional line: *You're already approved!*
Secret meaning: As long as you are willing to pay 21 percent interest, a $35 over-the-limit fee, and a $4,000 late charge, you are approved for credit. And we'll send you a free nail clipper.

Before you get excited about this type of professional line, you should know that creditors will also approve your two-month-old grandson, as long as he can drool a signature on the application form.

Service Professional line: *Perhaps your payment has crossed in the mail.*
Secret meaning: We're coming to get whatever you own. We will track you down. Repossession is in the works, so do not even try to hide.

Isn't it funny how nobody ever gets a notice that says, "By the way, you double-paid this month. Silly you. Here's your money back, along with a $35 overpayment credit"? No, they'll keep your extra payments and will still send you another statement the next month asking for more. And if you pay early, you won't get a thanks for that either. There's no "Good going, pal!" greeting in your next month's statement. Just the bill.

And have you noticed that whenever a utility bill suddenly drops, you will immediately hear from that company telling you that something must be wrong? Maybe it was an incorrect meter reading and they'll need to read it again, or perhaps there is a problem with your wiring, your pipes, or whatever else that might be causing you to have lower than normal readings. But when the reading quadruples in one month, they never suggest that *their* figures could be wrong.

Service Professional line: *Our delivery truck is on its way.*

Secret meaning: We have no idea where your package is. Your chances of ever receiving it are nil. What you will receive, however, is an inaudible cell phone call from a man who will be claiming that he's lost when in reality he is parked at the end of your block. He has been spying on your house, waiting for you to leave for the last three hours. As soon as you walk out your front door, get into your car and drive off, he will place a call to your home so that he'll be sure to get your answering machine. (Think about it. Are you ever at home when these deliverymen call? Of course not. And this is precisely why. It is a company's retaliation for the consumers' standard line, "The check's in the mail.")

When you return home and hear the answering machine message, and you call the company to ask about your package, they will have no record of you in their system. In fact, they will doubt you even exist, despite the fact that they are talking to you.

While we're on the subject of ordering things, what are these confirmation numbers that they give you? Those 15-digit numbers are treated as if they're supposed to mean something. The company representative will wait while you look all over the house for a piece of paper and a pen that works, then not only will he make you write it down, he'll make you repeat it back to him. But after you hang up, no one on the entire planet will ever ask you for that number again. It's simply a joke they're playing on us. They pull these numbers out of the sky, and once in a while they'll even throw in a letter just to make us really think it's legitimate. Proving our point yet again, some service professionals have way too much free time on their hands.

Case in point: Recently, I (Rick) got a delivery of a catalog order. To the workmen's surprise, I was at home when they called. The order was for a teakwood patio set. It had a Lazy Susan–style tray in the middle of the table, and we loved it. But when they shipped it, some of the pieces were missing. So I called the company to complain. Now, when you complain about something like that, what you expect, or rather hope, to hear them say is "I'm so sorry that you experienced a problem with your order. We can assure you that this is an unusual occurrence and we will do everything in our power to rectify the situation."

What you don't expect to hear them say is "Yeah, we've been having a lot of complaints about that product." Maybe it's just me, but if they're having a lot of complaints about a certain item, why don't they discontinue selling it until the problem can be fixed? Are they going to continue selling a product that they know they're going to get complaints about? If customers were finding baby alligators in the box that their pillows were being shipped in, you would think the company would either quit shipping the pillows or at least print a warning in the catalog about them. That way, only those of us who wanted an alligator with our pillows would order them.

Service Professional line: *Car repairs while you wait.*

Secret meaning: Do you really have that boring of a life that you have nowhere else to go and will willingly sit here all day and wait for your car to be repaired?

Addendum to the Secret meaning: We'll need to order the part you need, and you may be waiting four to six weeks, so we hope you brought deodorant.

Car repair shops never seem to have the right part. They're like the fake checkout stations at some super stores. Some auto repair shops will even have fake auto parts lining their walls and shelves just to trick you into thinking they have your part. But they don't. Of course.

Service Professional line: *Not everything is covered under our warranty.*

Secret meaning: Our warranty covers everything on your car that has a one in one billion chance of breaking. If it's covered under the warranty, you can bank on the fact that it will outlive you. What is not covered under the warranty is the engine, the electrical, the transmission, all windows including the windshield, the tires, and 95 percent of the rest of the vehicle.

While we're on the subject of cars, let's talk car insurance companies. Why is it that you can be with an insurance provider for twelve years, then get into an accident (not your fault). You need your bumper replaced, and they will immediately cancel your policy. They will even cancel you if it's starting to look like something could happen to you. "You were in the car with someone who got a ticket for going 35 in a 25-mile-per-hour zone. This increases your chances of being a speeder by 20 percent. We have no choice but to drop you."

Service Professional line: *How was your meal?*
Secret meaning: Don't complain to me; my shift's almost over. And besides, we've already handed out all the stomach pumps.

Service Professional line: *Lifetime warranty.*
Secret meaning: If you're a butterfly.

Service Professional line: *The cable should be back up and running in no time at all.*
Secret meaning: If you had any remote plans of watching your favorite shows, you might as well give them up and go on a week's vacation. There is only one guy fixing all the cable systems in your county. Like those super store checkout stations and the shelves of some auto parts stores, all those other cable trucks that you see around town are fake. As soon as you call the cable company, they will move one of these cars to your vicinity and park it, fooling you into thinking that they're fixing something just so you won't call them back. But it's an empty truck. A decoy. They are only trying to appease you.

When the cable does come back on, and it will eventually, I don't think anyone at the cable company truly knows why. It's like when your old television set used to go on the fritz. You would finally get so fed up that you would hit it with your hand, and suddenly the picture would come back on.

You had no idea why. It just came back on all by itself.

It's the same with cable. It'll just suddenly come back on even though no one really did anything to fix it. In fact, I challenge readers to call their cable company the next time their cable comes back on after a blackout and ask them how they managed to fix it. No one will be able to tell you.

Again, we do want to reemphasize that this code doesn't apply to all service professionals. Most service people are conscientious and care a great deal about customer satisfaction. These tales of woe are just about the ones we happen to run into. But then we get to make money writing about them, so I guess it all evens out in the end.

DEATH DOESN'T BECOME US

Most of us don't like to think about death. Especially our own. But let someone start talking about the subject, and before you know it, you're planning out your whole funeral. Before you know it, you and your wife are arguing over which family member is going to get to raise your children in the event you both die together. Before you know it, you're planning the menu for your memorial brunch.

This whole discussion of death, funerals, and post-funeral activities can get a little creepy. You're planning a family gathering knowing you're the only one who's not going to be getting any of the barbeque.

What's even more unsettling is when your wife starts picking out back-up wives for you, just in case she happens to go first. These are usually single friends of hers that she isn't the least bit jealous of. If she dies before you do, you are free to marry anyone from her pre-approved list. Even though you prefer someone with teeth.

I (Bubba) have to confess that Betty and I have selected possible subsequent spouses for each other. The choices aren't set in stone, but we have provided input to each other. I also have a few requests for my funeral. First of all, I want to have the song "Clocks" by Cold Play being played over the speakers while everyone is being seated. I think the song is appropriate because that will be the first time in my life that I will finally not have to answer to a clock.

I also want to open the memorial with a video of me talking to the audience. It would be pre-recorded, of course, sort of like what Yul Brenner did with those anti-smoking commercials. Only mine wouldn't be a public service announcement. I would just be interrupting the eulogy from time to time with funny little snide remarks about myself.

Sometime during the service, I envision "Amazing Grace" being played on bagpipes, like Mr. Spock had at his funeral in *Star Trek II—The Wrath of Khan*. The bagpipes can be off in the distance because, in the words of that great philosopher, Bugs Bunny, bagpipes can sometimes look like a monster attacking an old lady. I wouldn't want to scare any of the children.

I (Rick) have some thoughts about my funeral, too. An incident a few years ago made me realize that I could be a heart attack candidate if I didn't change a few things. So I did, and I feel great. Still, the episode has got me thinking about the worst-case scenario, and what if it were to happen. What would I want for my funeral?

First of all, I'm Southern Baptist so cremation is out of the question. At a Southern Baptist funeral you have to have a body because you have to have an after-funeral dinner. It's not necessarily sacrilege not to have a body at a Southern Baptist funeral, but it *is* sacrilege not to have a dinner.

Every good Southern Baptist knows that you cannot properly bury someone without plenty of potato salad, fried chicken livers, and homemade ice cream on hand. Here in the South, a funeral potluck is one of the biggest social events of the year.

As comedian James Gregory says, we Southerners go to the funeral and greet the bereaved with, "We're so sorry to hear about your loss, Deacon Carter. Here's a casserole."

Maybe it's me, but funeral food just seems to taste better than regular food. I don't know why that would be true, but it is. Unfortunately, Bubba and I are usually so distraught over whoever passed away, we can hardly eat that third plate.

And isn't it just like a good church member to plan their passing to coincide with the church's calendar?

"This weekend we'll be laying Sister Beulah Perkins to rest. It's also the Fourth of July weekend, so those of you with last names beginning with the letters A through L bring a meat dish, and those with last names beginning with the letters M through Z bring a dessert. The annual horseshoe tournament will begin right after the eulogy. God rest her soul."

But back to *my* funeral. I still have a few more requests. For all those planning the event, let me just say that I do not want an open casket. I wasn't that good looking when I was alive, so why would I want to be put on display after I'm gone? I don't feel like my color's going to be all that good on that day anyway. No one looks their best when they're dead. Which brings me to another point. Do you know here in the South, it's quite common for people to take pictures of the dearly departed in their coffin? Let me tell you, these photos can be a little jarring when you're going through someone's family album and suddenly you come across one. It's even worse if you see it made into a Christmas card.

As far as what I want to wear in the casket, that's easy. I want to be buried in my gym shorts and my "I Beat Anorexia" T-shirt. I want my earthly body to be comfortable. I won't actually be in it to complain, but I still want it to look comfortable.

Another point I'd like to bring up about funerals is why do people always say, "Oh, don't make a big fuss over me when I go"? Anybody who says they don't want a big fuss made at their funeral is lying. Everybody wants to be sent off in a big way. We all want to be missed. Did you know in the old days they used to have professional mourners? These were people you could rent to weep at your funeral. That's all they did. They would go to funerals and wail over the deceased. I'm not saying Sherri has to go to this extreme (although I do have a few weepers on retainer just in case), but I wouldn't mind a few tears shed over my passing.

Okay, I'm lying. I want *lots* of tears! I want a *huge* fuss made over me. I want about a thousand people there, and I want all of them so distraught they can hardly make it through the ceremony. I don't want it to end with a graveside interment either. I want Bubba to take my body on tour. I want it be a traveling memorial that'll roll through the entire southeast, including West Virginia and Missouri.

I should probably go ahead and announce (in case my kids are reading this) that I've decided that I'm not going to leave anything to my offspring either. They dried me out when I was alive; why should I let the practice continue beyond my demise? I'm just kidding, of course. Whatever I have is theirs. But I don't want it to be their focus. Do you realize how many people are living their entire lives focused on the money they are going to get after someone else in their family dies? Seems like a waste of precious time to me. Live with what you've got. If you inherit something later, fine. Enjoy it. The deceased wanted you to enjoy it. But first, enjoy the people around you who you love while they're alive. And tell them of your love as often as you can.

I'm not worried about my wife in a post-Rick world. I've got plenty of life insurance, so she will be filthy rich. And unlike Bubba and Betty, we haven't picked out the next spouse for each other after our deaths. I'll leave that to Sherri's own choice. Although, I would prefer that she not bring a date to the funeral (it's just in bad taste). She's a beautiful and wonderful woman, though, so I don't think she'll stay single long. But then again, we do have five kids, so she's going to have her work cut out for her finding my replacement.

Another request I have is that I don't want a hearse. I want them to use the show truck, the one with the words "Rick and Bubba" emblazoned on its side. It'll be like Elvis' funeral, only without the millions of fans. I also want sponsors. I want to have the first eulogy brought to you by Coca Cola.

I'm not above "guilting" some celebrity into doing my eulogy either. My first two choices would be Rush Limbaugh and Bill Cosby. I've been trying to get Rush on our radio show for years, but so far nothing's worked. Maybe my death is just the thing's he's been waiting for to commit. If not, I think Bill Cosby would be gracious enough to show up and say a few words. Either celebrity would be great.

I used to be in a band, and Bubba and I play from time to time, so I'd love to have some sort of musical performance at my funeral. Michael W. Smith would be good. Maybe a duet with Michael and Bubba.

The main thing is I want my funeral to be a celebration. I know where I'm spending my eternity. I'm secure in that. Certainly, there will be sadness if I die young and leave my wife and kids behind. But if that happens, I want them to have a party celebrating my life. I don't want anyone to hold back just because it's a funeral. I want them to tell funny stories, to laugh, and to have another piece of fried chicken. I don't want anyone dieting at my funeral. I want them to eat their portion and what I would have eaten, too.

Another request that I have for my funeral is that I be buried with my NCAA college video game from EA Sports. It's the only thing that was ever really mine. With five children and a wife, I don't have anything that is indisputably mine. I own nothing. Except my NCAA college video game.

As for my final resting place, after the memorial tour, I want my interment to be beneath the Big Boy statue at the radio station. Elvis was buried in his backyard, so I'm assuming you can get permits for this sort of thing somewhere. Maybe we can even have a photographer on hand who'll take pictures of tourists posing by Big Boy and standing on top of me. Of course, if *The Rick and Bubba Show* ever moves from Birmingham, Bubba would have to dig me up and take me with him. But he'd be willing to do that, I'm sure. After all, what are friends for?

THE RICK & BUBBA CODE TO LIFE

The Rick and Bubba Code to Life is simple truths that we have uncovered at some point in our lives. Some we've learned by watching others. Some we've known instinctively. And most we've learned in our usual manner—the hard way.

Here they are in no particular order, much like our expense accounts:

1. Being happy is a choice.

Every day we have choices to make. Paper or plastic, credit or cash, diet soda or banana split. That last one is a no-brainer. But we still have to order the banana split. It's not going to just come to us. As much as we'd like there to be one, there is no Baskin-Robbins genie.

Another one of the choices that we have to make is what kind of mood we are going to be in. That cranky lady you ran into at the mall made a choice to be cranky. That driver who honked his horn at you on your way to work yesterday made a choice to be impatient. That dietitian who told me to lose thirty pounds chose to be nitpicky. Our circumstances are often beyond our control, but the mood and attitude that we use to face them with is every bit in our control.

Far too many of us look to someone or something else to make us happy. We look to comedians, friends, our children or spouse, a new car, and who knows what else to make us happy. But real happiness happens inside of us.

I (Rick) was already happy when Sherri came along. I'm happier now, but I was already a happy person when we met. Bubba would say the same thing about himself when he met Betty. If you already have a base level of happiness, then when you're having a bad day, you can acknowledge it, admit that you have a right to be down, but decide to keep your joy in spite of your circumstances.

And order a second banana split.

2. Do less.

At the Burgess and Bussey households, we are committed to doing less. We don't have to be involved in every organized sport that comes along. We don't have to sign our kids up for all the service organizations within a three-county radius or get them lessons to learn how to play every musical instrument in the entire marching band. We don't have to spend so much time on our exercise equipment. (That last one was just to see if you were paying attention.)

A deacon friend of ours once told us that he remembers his kids asking him to tuck them into bed one night. He answered, "I'd love to go upstairs, kids, and tuck you in and pray with you, but I've got to go back to church and learn how to be a better father."

Now when he replays those words in his head he realizes how silly they sound. It's like signing up for a six-week course to learn how to have more free time.

It may look good to others that we're busy in school, church, Cub Scouts, Little League, and whatever else we have our kids signed up for; but are all these perfectly good activities really connecting us to our children? Or are our kids doing so many good things that the busyness is actually *keeping* us from cultivating a real relationship? Are we working so hard to give our kids everything they want and overlooking what they most need . . . us?

When's the last time you and your family had a day that you just did nothing? No plans, no location to rush to, no admission tickets to buy, no parking lot to maneuver your way around, no backseat feuds to referee. Nothing except getting to know each other a little better. Can you remember a day like that?

Maybe it's been years. Maybe you've never had one.

Someone once told a preacher that he shouldn't take a day off because the devil never rests. The preacher answered, "Yeah, but God did."

It's not a crime to take a break. To breathe. To sleep in and not get up until you are good and ready. To have a leisurely talk with your kids. Maybe even go for a walk or toss the football around in the backyard. Or attend your four-year-old daughter's tea party.

We weren't created to go 24/7. Just look at how many entertainers have collapsed after trying to meet some outrageous schedule. And they've got "people," but they still collapsed. The rest of us don't have "people" to schedule our activities or keep us from overcommitting and booking ourselves right out of our own lives.

Here's a weird concept for Americans: why not sit down and have dinner together with your family tonight? It could be enlightening. You might find out that the extra kid who's been living at your house for the past month-and-a-half actually belongs to one of the neighbors. You don't have to fund his college tuition after all.

Family dinners are a great time to connect, discuss school or life issues, pray together, have a good time. And eating with your family is one of the best ways to bond. Providing they don't beat you to seconds.

3. As much as possible, live your life so you have no regrets.

Regretting something from your past is wasted energy. You can't change anything about it now, so move on. Focus on the present and keep looking toward your future. Life is too important to waste on regrets or impossible-to-open shrink-wrapped packages.

4. Go on a date with your spouse at least once a week.

Be the parents your kids need to see. Moms, show love and respect to your children's father. Dads, love your children's mother. Both of these are not suggestions. They're biblical mandates. God tells us husbands to love our wives, and he tells wives to respect their husbands. Is this because we men are always doing everything right and are perfect, and that's why we deserve your respect? Of course not. It's because the position of husband and father deserves to be respected.

The two of us get invited to speak for a lot of different groups. Some of these gatherings can be quite large. But once Sherri asked me (Rick) to speak to a group that she belonged to. There were only about twenty-five people there, but I still gave the speech everything I had.

Afterward, when we got in the car, Sherri turned to me and said, "You did an outstanding job."

Now, in the kind of work we're in, we sometimes get paid a lot of compliments. Total strangers will come up to us and say, "I love your radio show," or, as we hope they do once this is published, "I love your book." But when you get that kind of a compliment from your wife, believe me, it's enough fuel to keep you going for quite a while. Respect means everything to a man.

Unfortunately, television and movies don't always show husbands and fathers in a positive light. Like we've said before when we were growing up we had *Father Knows Best, Andy Griffith,* and other shows with strong men who provided words of wisdom to their families. Now, in the days of Homer Simpson, men are confused. Down deep, they know that they were made to be strong and respected. It's who they are. But current culture has steadily chiseled away at some of that strength.

When a woman tears down her husband to others, she will never have the marriage she desires and deserves. The love she is seeking isn't going to come out of a man who isn't respected. If women could only grasp this truth, there might be fewer broken relationships. Respect, not food, is the key to a man's heart. But food does run a very close second.

5. Keep God #1 in your home and never ever give up.

No debate. Life and marriage are just a whole lot easier to handle when you've got all your priorities in order. And God is priority number one.

And no matter what comes your way, don't ever give up. We both have a saying that we shout out to our listeners on a regular basis. It's "Stay in it!" It means be unrelenting in what you believe. Stay the course. Don't just spin your tires. Go 100 percent in the direction of your dreams and goals and what you believe. Have principles that are unchanging. In other words, just "Stay in it!"

6. Better to make less doing something you love than make more doing something you hate.

We get a lot of invitations to luncheons and banquets, and we try to attend as many as we can. At least all the ones that let you take home a doggie bag. Recently, we received one that was going to have the president of the United States as the featured speaker. I (Bubba) knew I was taking my chances after what happened last time with Betty and the president, but then figured it was worth the risk. We had a table reserved for us, so I told my kids that I wanted them to go see and hear an actual sitting president. I was pretty excited, and so were the kids. But then Hunter walked over to the refrigerator where we keep the school lunch schedule and said, "I can't go Thursday. That's chicken fingers day."

Discover your passion. Right now, Hunter's passion is chicken fingers. Our passion is entertaining. Neither Rick nor I dread going to work tomorrow. We love what we do.

If you don't have a burning desire for the career you're currently pursuing, you might want to step back and take a little inventory of your life. What happened to your dreams, your desires, and your God-given talents? Are they being properly put to use?

We're not saying quit your job tomorrow. But seek God and see where you might be able to pursue some of your dreams. Maybe it's at your current job, but with new opportunities and responsibilities. Maybe it's in a different line of work. Maybe it's somewhere you never imagined.

Since I (Rick) was a kid I knew I was going to do something in entertainment. My school teachers used to try to scare me with, "So is this your plan, Rick Burgess? To just sit back and make funny comments all day long? You think that's going to carry you through life?"

Well. . . .

Little did I or they know then, but yes, that was exactly my plan. I didn't have a clue what I was going to do with my life, but something kept making me nurture a gift of humor that had been put inside of me; and no matter how hard I tried, I couldn't deny it was in there. I love to make people laugh. Bubba has the same gift hard-wired inside of him, too.

I wish we could say that once we discovered our gifts, we headed straight for the goal line. But we didn't. We both ended up taking several side trips before we made our way down the field. But even if a side trip slows down the game, it should never result in a forfeit. Get back on the field and play your hardest.

Will you be successful? How can you not be? When you're doing what you love, you're going to work hard at it. When you work hard at something, you can't help but improve and eventually end up doing it well. And because you're doing it well, you can't help but ultimately get rewarded with success.

We'll be the first to admit we're not the most talented guys in radio. But we've survived when others have failed because when they got discouraged and bailed, we kept coming in to work. In the Rick and Bubba Code, perseverance is the edge.

And on a side note, here's a good piece of advice. If you're going to go into business with a partner, you'd better be sure it's with someone you like. The two of us had a lot of fun back when we attended college together and we're still having fun today. We feel blessed to get to work together like this. We respect each other's talent, and we genuinely like each other. Our listeners can sense that.

7. Be forgiving.

No one gets through this life without saying their share of stupid things. And doing stupid things. We all make mistakes. Big ones, little ones, medium-sized ones. None of us is perfect. Don't fall into the self-righteous trap of holding other people to an unattainable goal.

If there is someone in your life that you need to resolve something with, be the bigger person and call him or her. You'll be doing it for you, so you can rest more peacefully at night.

We also realize you can't control others, though. Sometimes even when you reach out, the other person might not want to mend the relationship. That's his or her choice. But if we make the choice to forgive them, God says He'll forgive us.

What stops a lot of people from forgiving someone is the fear that their act of forgiveness will somehow mean the hurt wasn't real. Forgiveness doesn't mean that at all. It's not ignoring or dismissing the pain; it's facing real pain with amazing grace.

8. Don't just love someone, tell them you love them.

Just when you think you've told your spouse and children that you love them enough times to last them their whole lives, tell them again. Tell them all day long. You can never say it enough.

Don't assume they don't want to hear it. Everybody likes to hear that they're loved. We don't even mind a box of chocolates once in a while too.

9. Encourage others.

We don't encourage each other enough. Being strict is fine, but it needs to be tempered with unconditional love, understanding, and encouragement. That's how God is.

I (Rick) have the utmost respect for my father. Almost every week someone comes up to me and tells me how my dad changed his life. As a football coach, he could be hard. But the players always knew that he cared about them.

There are some parents who get the disciplinarian part down perfectly. But they don't have the rest of the package. And sometimes the rest of the package is the hardest part. It's not easy to love someone unconditionally. But it's the only way to truly love someone.

My son is currently involved in high school football. He comes from a long line of football players, football coaches, and football fans. Football is in our genes. But I've told him that what he does out on the field will never define our relationship. If he decides that football isn't for him, that's fine. If he decides that he loves the game and wants to go professional, that's fine with me, too. If he decides he would rather do Riverdancing, I'll keep buffing the hardwood floors and buy a set of earplugs. And maybe change my name. But I would be supportive. No matter what, I'm proud of him. On the field and off the field, when he does well and when he messes up, whichever it is, he's still my son.

Do you have any idea how freeing it is for our children to hear that truth—that our love for them doesn't depend on their performance? They need to know that they've already won our admiration and our hearts just by being who they are. The love part is already in the bank, regardless of performance.

Now, if we could just get our minds around the truth that this is exactly the way God feels about us.

10. Laugh more.

Be silly every chance you get. Life is a stumbling, bumbling comedy dance. None of us is going to get all the steps right. But we can still enjoy the music and have a good time. So fill your day with as many laughs as you can. Look for unexpected joys in life, and whatever you do, don't take yourself so seriously. After all, if we're really honest with ourselves, our own habits, quirks, and missteps are enough to keep us laughing for a lifetime. If you never make mistakes and your life is completely and boringly perfect, it may be time for a reality check. Ask those around you to tell you to point out some of your flaws. It probably won't take them half as long as you think it will to come up with one or two. Or more. But don't take it personally. You're in good company. And anyway, if it's healthy to laugh at yourself, you might as well have plenty of material to draw from. Why do you think we went into comedy?

EPILOGUE

Same Undisclosed Radio Station, Alabama
Some time later

Speedy awoke with a sudden jerk. Apparently, it had all been a dream.

Everything. All of it. A dream. He knew he should have been working, but since Rick and Bubba were asleep in the studio, he too felt justified in getting a few hours of sleep. The football jersey beside him bore the monogram THE RICK AND BUBBA SHOW. He looked at it and wondered, what day is it?

When he glanced up at the calendar, he realized that he had actually been asleep for two days. Nothing unusual there. But then he realized what had jerked him awake. It was a thought that had come into his head, the oddest thought.

Could it be so?

He rolled over and thought about it some more.

Impossible. It couldn't be true.

The revelations were coming now, fast and furious. Bubba's ancient spelling of "deep fried," the Big Gulp cup on the desk, the station walls covered with portraits of Rick and Bubba on velvet, painted by a master, as well as the presidential photographs and the one of the fish fry. It was all *making some sort of twisted sense. That's why Rick and Bubba had avoided him last week at lunch. It had nothing to do with their not wanting to get stuck with the check. (Okay, maybe a little.)*

Had they avoided him because he had unknowingly stumbled onto the truth of The Rick and Bubba Code*?*

Speedy ran down the long hallway of the radio station and into the parking lot. Out of breath, he lifted his eyes and gazed upon the statue before him—Big Boy. What could it mean?

Is this why Bubba had wanted to leave work early all week? All month for that matter? Is this why Rick kept playing games on his cell phone? Maybe they weren't games. Maybe he was ordering pizzas. Maybe it wasn't his cell phone at all. Maybe it was Bubba's, and Bubba would now get stuck with the cell phone bill. And the bill for the pizzas.

Had Speedy unintentionally stumbled onto the truth?

With a feeling of wonder and an undeniable weakness from hunger, Speedy fell to his knees. It all had to mean something. But what? What?

For a minute, he thought he heard a woman's voice . . . the woman from the pizza delivery service . . . whispering something to him from behind a stack of pizza boxes that now towered in front of her. She seemed to be saying just one simple message, a secret message from Rick and Bubba to every generation past and to every generation yet to come . . .

"Stay in it, people!"

Rick & Bubba, Take Us Away!

Looking for a healthy way to pass what precious free time you have between your job, your family, your church, and whatever else you've got going on in your life? Have we got the mental vacation spot for you! Pack up your worries and cruise on over to the Rick and Bubba Web site at **www.rickandbubba.com**.

At **www.rickandbubba.com** you'll get in on all the latest Rick and Bubba news. You'll be able to order their brand-new (and previously released) CDs and DVDs and even subscribe to Rick and Bubba's X-treme Access, which gives you access to all the video clips, audio bits, and the archives of their daily show for a full six months from the date of activation. Imagine having all those wacky "on location" moments, special celebrity guest visits, crazy in studio segments, live Mr. Lucky recordings, and rare footage from the Rick & Bubba video vault just a mouse click away. Be the first to witness rare, never-before-aired bloopers! And it's all commercial free!

We post information on our upcoming radio guests, as well as information on booking Rick and Bubba for a special guest appearance at your next community event or church gathering (potluck required). Okay, we're joking about the potluck. It's recommended, not required.

At **www.rickandbubba.com** you'll get to meet the staff of the Rick and Bubba show through a fun photo gallery. We even list the Rick and Bubba upcoming personal appearances, and where you can catch the next Mr. Lucky (the official Rick and Bubba band) show live. You'll also find updates on the Rick and Bubba Softball Team, as well as Web site links to some of our friends.

Now, we ask you, does all that sound like fun to you? Of course it does! So don't waste another day! As soon as you finish reading this book (you've still got a few more pages to go), escape to Rick and Bubba's Web site and give yourself a long overdue comedy break.

www.rickandbubba.com — That's the only secret code you need!

THE HISTORY OF RICK & BUBBA

Rick and Bill (as Bubba was known then) went to rival high schools (Rick went to Oxford High in Oxford, Alabama, and Bill went to Jacksonville High, in Jacksonville, Alabama.). The two became friends when they both found themselves attending the same university, Jacksonville State University, and working at the college radio station there. This was back in Rick's long-haired, rock-'n'-roll singing, afternoon radio guy days. Bill was the promotions director and engineer (they wouldn't let him have a shift other than the graveyard shift because of his strong Southern accent. The powers that be felt it was difficult to understand what he was saying. Apparently, that rule didn't apply to some of the bands they would play.)

After college, Rick went on to a maze of broadcasting jobs at WHMA-AM and FM, then on to a new '80s and '90s docket station WKFN now WVOK-FM in his hometown of Oxford, Alabama, while continuing to tour some with his band. Bill continued to work behind the scenes in radio. He began a career in directing the newscast at WJSU-TV in Anniston, Alabama, and a part time job at WPID in Piedmont, Alabama (where they would actually let him talk on the air!). Bill ended up as chief engineer for WQEN/WAAX in Gadsden, Alabama. When management was looking for a new morning man, Bill wasted no time recommending Rick for the job.

While working together, Rick and Bill enjoyed hanging out and creating new ideas for the show. One day at lunch, Bill said "Are you going to eat those fries?" But then he also said, "Wouldn't it be funny if you read Shakespeare in a country voice and called it Good Ole Boy Theater!" The next morning with Bill looking in, Rick prepared to do it. But then, about thirty seconds before the break was over, Rick told Bill, "You sit down and do it!" So Bill did! It was a hysterical bit, and Rick said "You sound like my Uncle Bubba". And Bill "Bubba" Bussey was born. Not only did the new name stick, but before long, Bubba was sitting in for a few minutes a day every day. Ultimately, he started sticking around for the whole show. The listeners would not have it any other way. The teaming of Rick and Bubba was a huge success. Rick had said he always wanted a partner, but he just couldn't find the right person. Bubba was it. And Bubba says he's honored to work with someone as talented and funny as Rick. Under new guidance and leadership, the team moved like a mighty army across the fruited plain. It turns out all their joking around in college has finally paid off. And if ratings don't lie, it would seem that Bubba has a pretty good radio voice after all.

BREAKING NEWS!

STILL LOOKING FOR A CANDIDATE THAT YOU CAN GET EXCITED ABOUT?

TIRED OF THE SAME OLD BORING DEBATES AND CAMPAIGN SPEECHES?

READY FOR A CHANGE, BUT AREN'T SURE EXACTLY WHAT KIND OF CHANGE?

WELL, HOLD ONTO YOUR CHAD!

THAT'S RIGHT, THE PUBLISHERS AND THE ENTIRE RICK AND BUBBA TEAM ARE PROUD TO ANNOUNCE THAT RICK AND BUBBA HAVE FORMALLY DECIDED TO TOSS THEIR BASEBALL CAPS INTO THE RING FOR THE *CO-PRESIDENCY OF THE UNITED STATES!*

WHY WOULD THEY DO THIS? WHY NOT? AFTER ALL, IF WASHINGTON IS GOING TO KEEP GIVING US AS MUCH COMEDY MATERIAL AS IT DOES, THEY FIGURE IT'S THEIR KIND OF TOWN!

BUT WHY A CO-PRESIDENCY, YOU ASK? WELL, WE HAD IT BEFORE WITH THE CLINTONS, SO WHY NOT TRY IT AGAIN?

RICK AND BUBBA WILL BE OUR KIND OF CO-PRESIDENTS. THEY'LL BE IN IT FOR THE COMMON MAN. NO MORE WASTING TAXPAYER'S MONEY ON FANCY WHITE HOUSE DINNERS. THEY SAY, LET THE QUEEN EAT BARBEQUE! AND WHO'S TO SAY A RACK OF BABY BACK RIBS AND SOME POTATO SALAD WON'T PUT NORTH KOREA'S KIM JONG II IN A LOT BETTER MOOD?

OUR FELLOW AMERICANS, THE ONLY POLITICAL ADVERTISEMENT YOU'RE GOING TO NEED THIS ELECTION SEASON IS YOUR OWN COPY OF *RICK & BUBBA FOR PRESIDENT*, IN WHICH THEY TACKLE THE BIG ISSUES:

- **PRESIDENTIAL DINNERS**
- **WHITE HOUSE DÉCOR**
- **FOOD AND DRUG ADMINISTRATION AND WHY FATS GET A BAD WRAP**
- **TAXES**
- **PRESIDENTIAL SECURITY (CUSTOMIZING AIR FORCE ONE)**
- **CONGRESS' WORST LAWS ON THE BOOKS**
- **FOREIGN AFFAIRS AND BARBEQUE DINNERS**
- **FREE TRADE FOR RICK & BUBBA CDS**

IMAGINE IT—RICK'S KIDS PLAYING IN THE LINCOLN BEDROOM. ANOTHER BUBBA IN THE WHITE HOUSE. BOTH OF THEM RUNNING THE RISK OF GETTING THE NUCLEAR CODE MIXED UP WITH THEIR PERSONAL CHECKING ACCOUNT PASSWORDS. GIVEN THE GROWING POPULARITY OF RICK AND BUBBA, A CAMPAIGN FOR A CO-PRESIDENCY WAS INEVITABLE. SOME SAY IT'S LONG OVERDUE.

Rick & Bubba For President

"PRAISE FOR *RICK & BUBBA'S* EXPERT GUIDE TO GOD, COUNTRY, FAMILY AND ANYTHING ELSE WE CAN THINK OF"

Rick and Bubba are two of the most talented people on radio today. I am proud to call them my friends and look forward to the day when their show blankets the nation!

—*Sean Hannity*, Syndicated radio host and co-host of *Hannity & Colmes* on FOX News

Need a reason to smile or thought to ponder? Rick and Bubba provide them daily to hundreds of thousands. This delightful team blends down-home humor with rock-solid truth. I love them!

—*Max Lucado, New York Times* best-selling author

Rick and Bubba have filled *Rick and Bubba's Expert Guide to God, Country, Family, and Anything Else We Can Think Of* with the energy, optimism, and southern hospitality that makes their radio show such a blast.

—*Newt Gingrich*

I have had a chance to travel the country and hear hundreds of radio teams, and I cannot find a more powerful and entertaining duo than Rick and Bubba. These guys not only know the issues, but make it funny. And did I mention they have a few opinions?

—*Brian Kilmeade*, FOX News Channel co-host of *Fox & Friends* and author of *The Games Do Count*

Rick and Bubba are two of the funniest, happiest, nicest people on the planet. *Rick and Bubba's Expert Guide to God, Country, Family and Anything Else We Can Think Of* is every bit as good as their fast-paced radio show—and a great reminder why most Americans are optimists!

—*Oliver North*, Lt. Col., USMC (ret.)

Rick & Bubba's
Expert Guide to
GOD, COUNTRY, FAMILY
AND ANYTHING ELSE WE CAN THINK OF

ISBN 0-8499-0992-9